NO MATTER H...
home-baked bread puts the commercial
variety to shame! No wonder there's a
growing enthusiasm for bread-baking
—it's a healthy reaction against the
artificiality in our food and the
harmful additives they keep sneaking
into our lives.

Here's everything you need to know
to get you started. Discover what a
joyful, rewarding experience it is to

Bake Your Own Bread
And Be Healthier

"At last. A down-with-the-mystique-of-bread-
making book that does just that."—*Houston
Chronicle* ·

"A must for both health food enthusiasts and
traditional cooks."—*Florida Times-Union*

*Happy Birthday
Helen*

x x

Alice

Other SIGNET Books You'll Enjoy

Bake
Your
Own
Bread
And
Be
Healthier

Floss and Stan Dworkin

A SIGNET BOOK

NEW AMERICAN LIBRARY

TIMES MIRROR

SIGNET, SIGNET CLASSICS,
SIGNETTE, MENTOR and PLUME BOOKS are
published by The New American Library, Inc.,
1301 Avenue of the Americas, New York,
New York 10019

First Printing, October, 1973

3 4 5 6 7 8 9

PRINTED IN THE UNITED STATES OF AMERICA

Contents

Bread baking is a lot like married love.
The first loaves of bread you make are not
the best you'll ever make, but they're better
than any you've ever bought.

PREFACE

Why We
No Longer
Use Margarine

Since finishing the manuscript for this book almost two years ago we've had second and third thoughts about the question of margarine versus butter.

Margarine was so much cheaper than butter, we used to keep it in the house for my baking classes. Well, that lower price is no bargain.

Butter is made from cream, a highly saturated fat. By churning, air is forced into this fat to make it solid. Sometimes salt is added (originally, no doubt, to preserve it, now because so many consumers are used to the flavor). Sometimes, especially in the winter when there is nothing green for our northern cows to eat, coloring is added to give it the look of summer cream (yellowish) rather than the look of winter cream (off-white). You can tell this colored butter because it does look so yellow—but there is no warning on the label. Undyed butter is widely available.

Margarine is a combination of vegetable oils and other ingredients—often, several chemicals. The oil used is usually not identified. Corn and soya oil are widely used and these unsaturated oils (if not tampered with) are good food. If, however, it is cottonseed oil, DDT residues may remain, because cotton, not considered a food crop, is heavily sprayed. If it is coconut oil, it is a very saturated oil to start with. This combination of oil and chemicals (and such other stuff as milk powder, salt, and water) is then hydrogenated (air is forced into it and the empty links of the molecules are filled by hydrogen) to make it solid—as solid as butter and as saturated as butter, and then dyed to make it look like butter.

There are so-called soft margarines, which contain more unsaturated oil—but often more chemicals. These too are dyed.

Neither butter nor margarine is essential to your diet. Some unsaturated fat is needed for those oil-soluble vitamins and for skin and hair tone.

Originally, we felt that either butter or margarine could be used for greasing the pans in our recipes. We have come to the conclusion that we were mistaken, and while it is too late to reset the type for all the recipes in *Bake Your Own Bread*, it is not too late to include this preface.

We now feel that the chemicals and dyes in margarine constitute a danger, and so we recommend that only butter be used to grease your baking pans.

To repeat: where our recipes read "For Greasing, melted butter or margarine," use melted butter only.

☞ 1 ☜

Down
with
the
Mystique

À BAS LE MYSTIQUE

Over the years a mystique has grown up around bread baking; a kind of mystery (in the old Greek sense of a secret religious society) which excluded the outsider who hadn't learned the rites at her mother's knee. Recently, however, there has been a renaissance of interest in home baking—probably a reaction to much of the artificiality in our food and a desire to eliminate some of the additives they keep sneaking into our lives. This interest in baking is part of the overall growth in interest in improving the quality of what goes into our stomachs.

This guide to the perplexed will steer you through the simplicities of bread baking, and through the complexities of improving your diet through baking your own bread.

It is not everything you ever wanted to know about baking but couldn't find out from your mother. Rather, it provides a foundation of techniques and recipes which, once mastered, will enable you to go on to virtually any bread, inventing recipes of your own, or adapting standard recipes to greater wholesomeness, improving your own and your family's health.

As for the mystique—there is none. Bread baking is a simple process, easily learned, quickly mastered by woman, man, or child, a satisfying and delicious pastime, a rewarding addition to everyday cooking, even profitable if you have the business sense.

Furthermore, bread you bake yourself is free from the chemical additives and free from the dirt introduced in any commercial bakery. (See Appendix B.)

Before going on to the recipes themselves, let me introduce you to the ingredients I use, to tell you where and how they fit into bread baking, and how they fit into a healthier diet.

THE INGREDIENTS

Flours

The flours and meals you'll be using in these recipes are the finely ground berries of various grasses (wheat, rye, corn) and beans (soy).

There are many other flours: buckwheat, barley, millet, peanut, ginseng, rice, even fish flour (not available in the States), to list a few. Any could be substituted for part of the flour listed in the recipes (you'll read about substitutions later on).

However, this is not a comprehensive but a basic book, and, basically, we'll be using wheat flour (white and whole), rye, corn, and soy.

WHEAT

The wheat berry (like all the grass berries) is made up of three parts: the coarse outer layer, the bran; the embryo or wheat germ (the part that, given the chance, would sprout into a new plant); and the inner part, or endosperm.

In the bran there are many vitamins and minerals, and proteins of a high quality (that is, proteins that are readily used by the body for the vital processes).

In the germ we have one of the richest sources of vitamin E, which is necessary for the absorption of vitamin A, and for general vitality. Experiments show that a lack of E can lead to heart disease. The germ also contains vitamin B, high-quality proteins, and oil high in food value and a good source of lecithin.

The endosperm is mostly starch with very little protein. It contains virtually no vitamins and minerals.

White flour is made exclusively of the endosperm.

When millers remove the bran and the germ from flour, they remove about twenty-five vitamins and minerals. When they enrich the flour before marketing it, they return *four* vitamins—and three of those in *smaller amounts than what was removed.*

Why?

Profit. And consumer preference.

In the mid-nineteenth century, when the invention of new milling techniques made it possible to produce white flour—prior to that, man was technologically too primitive to impoverish the food he ate—it was discovered that this new flour made a bread much finer in texture than whole wheat. There was an immediate demand for this "better" flour by the rich. (The poor took a while to catch up.) Millers and shopkeepers preferred it, too, because the removal of the germ meant that the white flour could be kept longer, there being nothing "live" left in it to go rancid.

After removal of the bran and germ came bleaching—a process wherein a gas is forced through the flour to whiten it further (and, incidentally, kill any last trace of vitamin E, etc., that might have remained).

The Minnesota Agricultural Experiment Station did an interesting experiment in the late 1940s. They took healthy, grain-fed cattle and began to feed them on grain from which the germ (and therefore the vitamin E) had been removed. The cattle continued to *look* just as healthy, but they began to drop dead of heart disease! After a while, the experimenters restored them to their former diet of whole grain. There were no more deaths from heart disease.

However, for all its nutritional deficiencies, there is no question that white flour gives you a finer textured bread than whole wheat does. It is lighter, fluffier, less absorbent, easier to shape, and easier to rise. I tried, as an experiment, to make Brioches with whole wheat flour. The flavor was good—but the texture? It just wasn't Brioches. The same is true of Challah—and of other light, airy breads as well. They were invented for white flour and, if whole wheat is used instead, they come out different breads.

What to do?

Our solution is to substitute raw wheat germ for some of the flour in every white bread we bake. (Our everyday bread is 100 percent whole wheat, or whole wheat mixed with other whole grains.)

In the recipes that call for white flour, use un-bleached white flour—it, at least, has no chemical residues in it from bleaching, and does have a slightly higher vitamin content. After you learn the texture and feel of breads in their easiest form, I hope that you, too, will substitute raw wheat germ or whole wheat flour routinely for part of the white flour.

Wheat flour comes in several varieties:

Whole wheat or graham flour. This should contain all the bran and all the germ. It is rich in B and E vitamins and contains many other nutrients. Sometimes you find a cheaty graham flour, which is white flour with a little bran thrown back. This is better than straight white, but it is far from whole wheat.

Whole wheat flour should be *stone ground*—which means that instead of being ground by high-speed (high-heat) steel grinders, which tend to leave the wheat germ oil in biggish clumps (and kill the vitamin E), the wheat berries are ground between stone wheels which grind the germ and oil particles up finely and distribute them better throughout the flour. This helps the flour to keep longer without going rancid.

Rancidity is a problem with whole wheat flour (and all whole grain flours). You must sniff it when you buy it—if it's off you can smell it. If possible, store flour in the refrigerator to help keep it fresher. If, after you wet it with the other ingredients, it smells rancid, throw it out. Never eat flour that has gone bad; rancid oils have a remarkable power to destroy vitamins.

Two caveats: (1) Be certain your source of flour is a reliable one, and is not (as happened to me in a popular health food store) selling you vitamin E-less, chemical-ized, steel-ground whole wheat as the more expensive and healthier stone ground. (2) Be certain that the whole wheat flour you buy is not bleached or brominated. Brom-inating (exposure of the flour to bromine gas) destroys the germ, and so, much of the nutritive value. Pillsbury, for example, markets a brominated graham flour.

Wheat germ flour. This is unbleached, enriched white flour with the wheat germ returned after milling. Nutritionally it is quite good, and some brands come from Deaf Smith County, in Texas, where the mineral content of the soil makes for especially nutritious grains. The only trouble with this kind of flour is that it tends to be quite expensive. You can make your own wheat germ flour by using unbleached enriched white flour and substituting raw wheat germ as described in the recipes.

Unbleached enriched white flour. This flour gives you all the textural advantages of bleached flour without having gone through that last chemical treatment. It is only slightly more nutritious than bleached flour, but it is free of the chemical residues that bleaching can leave.

Bleached enriched white flour. As I said above, in this flour some twenty-five nutrients have been removed, and four returned, and they call that enrichment! There is also an unenriched white flour, but unless you have access to a commercial bakery, you shouldn't come into contact with it. Nutritionally it's on a par with library paste. And until recent pressure was brought by the federal government on the large companies, this nutrition-free junk was what all children's cakes were made of. Now, after being forced to add enrichment, the companies advertise: "Now Enriched!" as if they'd done something wonderful.

Gluten flour. "Gluten" is the protein part of the wheat berry, and gluten flour is about 50 percent protein. (Much of the starch has been removed.) It is usually reserved for people on special diets (diabetics, for example).

The gluten is that part of the flour which, by rubbing against itself in kneading, forms an elastic substance that holds the bubbles that the yeast makes. That's how yeast bread rises: by the elastic holding the expanding carbon dioxide bubbles released by the yeast. However, there are many flours that don't have any or much gluten—soy, for example. So, when I want to use a lot of soy (or any nongluten) flour in a recipe, I make sure to include some gluten flour to balance it out.

This flour does not have a good texture, but it can serve a good purpose.

Other wheat flours. If you shop around the health food stores (or mail order catalogues) you might well come across three other varieties of wheat flour: *whole wheat pastry flour, cracked wheat,* and *wheat grits.* All three of them are whole wheat (and so, good foods); all three of them are *not* suited to bread baking.

Whole wheat pastry flour is made from a different variety of wheat than the flour we use for bread baking. Also, it is more finely ground. If you try to make bread from it, the breads *will not rise,* and will have a "strange" flavor. You can use it for cookies, puddings, gravies, pastries, that sort of thing, but not bread.

Cracked wheat is the wheat berry cracked into large chunks, and you might as well try to knead bird gravel. While it is unsuitable as the *only* flour in a bread, it does make a nice textural addition—as does wheat grits (the wheat berry broken into smaller pieces). The commercial cracked wheat bread is made of white flour with some, though not much, cracked wheat added to it.

RYE

Rye is a very tasty flour, with very little gluten. A bread with a great deal of rye will have difficulty rising. One virtue of rye is that because it is not in great demand, it is available, I believe, only as a whole, stone-ground grain, unbleached, unenriched, unmucked about with in any way. But don't take my word for it. Read that label. If it doesn't say "stone ground" it's not stone ground. If it doesn't say "whole" or "100 percent whole" then something has been removed.

Rye also comes as a meal—a coarser grind of the same grain. If you can get it, do so, and use it instead of rye flour. The textural change is delightful.

CORN

There are cornmeals which are actually corn flours—the difference, again, is in the fineness of the grinding. The finer the grind, the more likely it is that the cornmeal will completely dissolve in the baking, leaving its flavor but not its texture.

Buying cornmeal can be tricky. For the most part, the cornmeals sold in supermarkets are enriched *degerminated.* They say it right on the box, "degerminated," in big letters, as if they were proud of it.

The germ of the corn—as the germ of the wheat or the rye—is the healthful part. If the germ is removed, all that is left are empty calories and a sprinkling of protein (not much, and poor-quality protein at that).

There is available in the supermarkets a brand of

white cornmeal that is stone ground and not degerminated: Indian Head. Of course, the health food stores
carry stone-ground yellow cornmeal that is complete.

SOY

As mentioned before, soy is not a grass like wheat or corn
or rye, it is a legume and, aside from gluten flour, the best
source of protein of any flour I use (about 40 percent protein). For vegetarians and others who don't eat much in
the way of animal proteins, soybeans are very important
in the diet because, like animal proteins, soybean proteins
are "complete."

When buying soy flour you have to watch out for
"defatted" or "low fat:" Again, it is the oil (or fat) that
carries the lecithin (nutritionally very important); but
even low-fat soy flour is a good food.

Yeasts

Yeasts have been used by man since the dawn of his-
tory—and probably earlier. All fermented drinks are
changed from carbohydrate-rich liquids to part-alcoholic
liquids by yeasts. Robert Graves says that beer goes back
to pre-Hellenic times.

The Bible records that in the desert the children of
Israel had to make do with unleavened bread—so, clearly,
they usually ate leavened (yeast-risen) bread. The yeast
that rose their bread was of the wild or sourdough variety (see Chapter 5).

Skipping down the ages to relatively modern times,
brewers have kept their strains of yeast alive for genera-
tions—they are part of what give various beers their different flavors. For many years brewer's yeast was what
Grandma baked with—she simply went to the brewer
and bought a chunk.

Brewer's yeast (and a related strain called torula
yeast) is very high in B vitamins and protein. When dried
(and no longer alive) it is used as a dietary supplement,
an excellent idea these days when it's all but impossible
to get a broad range of B vitamins in our diet.

By the late nineteenth century Grandma was able to
buy prepackaged cake yeast, a live strain related, but not
identical, to brewer's yeast, with the yeast living in a

dryish—for yeast—medium that was mostly starch. By keeping this cake yeast as cool and dry as she could, she was able to keep a supply of it in her kitchen—until it went moldy.

One of the technological miracles to come out of World War II (along with DDT and nerve gas) was *active dry yeast*, which lasts for years in a dormant state (so long as it is kept dry: wetting it brings it to life).

Active dry yeast is superior in every way to cake yeast.

Cake yeast lives in its food and *is alive*—which means that unless you use it promptly either the yeast will eat all its food and die, or mold will take over. Active dry yeast is *dormant*, so may be kept for years.

Cake yeast is sensitive to temperature, doing its best at about the heat of tepid water, and being killed off by too much heat. Active dry yeast is operative through a broad range of temperatures—approaching 180°! This means that you can use quite hot liquid to start with, which in turn means much *faster* and *stronger* yeast action.

Cake yeast must be mashed in liquid and dissolved before it's ready to go into your recipe. Active dry yeast can be measured right into the bowl with the other ingredients; it begins working as soon as you add some liquid.

Cake yeast must be "proved": that is, after mashing and dissolving, it must be watched for bubbling, to make certain that it's still alive. With active dry yeast, there's no such problem.

So in all those old recipes (including Grandma's) that call for cake yeast, substitute! Where it says a cake of yeast, use a tablespoon of active dry yeast; Grandma will never know the difference.

(If, after all this, you insist on using cake yeast—and heaven knows there are stubborn people in this world—remember: 1 cake of yeast equals 1 tablespoon of dry; the cake must be mashed and proved; and all the liquids in the recipe must be lukewarm.)

I do offer this caution about active dry yeast.

I used to tell my students that there was no difference between either of two active dry yeasts: Fleischmann's, which was more expensive, but premeasured and in dated aluminum packets; and El Molino, available in quarter-pound to pound packages and thus much cheaper, but requiring refrigeration once the cellophane package was opened. Well, it's no longer true. Fleischmann's has taken to using a preservative in their yeast (why a preservative in a sealed packet of dried yeast, I can't imagine)—BHA, one of the preservatives restricted in England but not here. And I can only *dis*-recommend anything with chemical preservatives.

If you can't find El Molino yeast at a health food store near you, write for their catalogue: El Molino Mills, Alhambra, California. (Walnut Acres, Penns Creek, Pennsylvania, also sells a nonpreserved yeast in bulk.)

Sweeteners

COMPOSITION OF FOODS (100 GRAMS)

	Granulated sugar	Honey	Blackstrap molasses
Food energy (calories)	385	304	213
Protein (gm)	0	0.3	0
Carbohydrates (gm)	99.5	82.3	55
Calcium (mg)	0	5	684
Phosphorous (mg)	0	6	84
Iron (mg)	0.1	0.5	16.1
Sodium (mg)	1	5	96
Potassium (mg)	3	51	2,927
Thiamin (mg)	0	trace	0.11
Riboflavin (mg)	0	0.04	0.19
Niacin (mg)	0	0.3	2.0
Vitamin C (mg)	0	1	0

Based on U.S. Department of Agriculture Handbook No. 8, Composition of Foods.*

Before I say word one about sweeteners, make sure you've cast an eye at the preceding table.

The federal government bears me out—white sugar is, to all intents and purposes, *nutrition-free*. It has cal-

* Send $2 to: Superintendent of Documents, U.S. Government Printing Office, Washington, D.C. 20402. It's very worthwhile.

ories, it is almost pure carbohydrate, and *it is then value-less as a food.* In addition, once in your system, it will destroy B vitamins.

I urge you in the strongest terms possible to eliminate sugar entirely from your diet. My husband and I have.

We use only two sweeteners—for baking, cooking, desserts, beverages, everything—honey and blackstrap molasses.

HONEY

Honey is nectar gathered from flowers by bees (different flowers give you different flavors), predigested by the bees, and then evaporated by them to the thick consistency with which you're familiar. It is this predigestion which gives it unique properties. For example, honey can be digested by a stomach too damaged or too sensitive to digest anything else.

Honey has a flavor that far surpasses sugar, and contains in addition small amounts of a wide range of vitamins and minerals—as well as having a *natural preservative power* that can keep your breads fresher quite a long while. Commercial bakers are aware of this preservative power, and you will find commercial breads that contain honey among their ingredients—and no artificial preservatives. Sweet breads and cakes made with large amounts of honey can be stored indefinitely.

There are many therapeutic claims made for honey: I know several beekeepers who insist that honey keeps them well and young; other beekeepers have described its curative powers quite convincingly, and my husband has successfully used it as an antiseptic on several occasions.

BLACKSTRAP MOLASSES

Blackstrap molasses is closely related to the granulated sugar that can destroy vitamins in the body. They both come out of the same pot, so to speak.

There is nothing wrong with cane sugar in the cane. It has many vitamins and minerals and, aside from wreaking havoc on the teeth, might be highly recommended. However, once that cane sugar is harvested and thrown into the pot for boiling down, what happens is this: the heavier particles, the ones that contain the minerals, sink to the bottom. From the topmost layer—the nutrition-free layer—they take sugar, crystallize it, "refine" it further, and granulate it. This is the valueless part.

From the next layer, they take light molasses—still not worth much nutritionally. From the next layer they take a darker (better) grade of molasses. And from the bottom layer they take blackstrap. It's this bottom layer that contains all the nutritional goodies—huge amounts of all the good minerals and all the vitamins except those that are heat-sensitive.

You can find the lighter grades of molasses in all supermarkets, and the blackstrap in all health food stores. If you decide to buy a lighter grade, at least make certain that you get unsulfured molasses. The sulfuring is a chemical additive that does you no good.

Blackstrap molasses will not extend the freshness of your bread, but it has other remarkable properties: aside from liver, there is no richer natural source of iron available to us, and blackstrap contains traces of copper, which enables the body to absorb that iron; apart from the food values in the table, which show blackstrap also to be a good source of B vitamins (absent from most foods), blackstrap also contains a very wide range of minerals which it's almost impossible to get elsewhere—all this with only two thirds the calories and almost half the carbohydrates of sugar.

Blackstrap molasses has a licorice flavor that doesn't appeal to everyone; however, it's a taste well worth acquiring, and, when used in baking, a taste that disappears into the whole.

OTHER SWEETENERS

There are other sweeteners you may run across in your shopping:

"Raw" or Turbinado sugar. The only thing raw about this is the deal you get. This is sugar with a tiny bit of the minerals re-added—all of 2 percent. That's right, Turbinado sugar is 2 percent better than white sugar—at about three times the price.

Brown sugar. This comes in two grades, light and dark. This sugar is slightly better than white because the color is gotten by adding some molasses to the refined sugar—but then why not use molasses?

Maple sugar. This is quite rich in minerals, but very expensive and not widely available. If you can find it and afford it, by all means use it.

Molasses—other grades. As I said, blackstrap isn't the only grade of molasses. There are two other grades (light and dark—with the dark more nutritious than the light), neither of which is as good as blackstrap, but both of which are tremendously better than white sugar, and there is Barbados molasses, which is absolutely delicious and has virtually no food value (hardly better than white sugar).

In adapting other people's recipes, remember that all sweeteners are interchangeable. If it says 2 tablespoons of sugar, you can substitute 2 tablespoons of honey or of blackstrap. (Actually, honey is slightly sweeter than sugar, so 0.9 honey for 1 sugar would be more accurate.)

You can substitute blackstrap for the honey in any of my recipes that call for a tablespoon or two of honey without much affecting the flavor, but you will affect the color—blackstrap darkens a batter.

Milk

Calcium absorption takes place only in the presence of fat, therefore, children should have whole milk. If a child drinks whole milk, the fat is right there and there is no problem of absorption. If a child drinks nonfat milk, how does he manage calcium absorption?

Just what is whole milk? Certainly not the stuff that passes for whole milk in your supermarket dairy case. Americans stopped drinking really whole milk when pasteurization pushed raw milk off the commercial market.

There were good reasons for pasteurization—what with the diseases that could be spread through milk—but there were alternatives that were ignored because pasteurization was commercially feasible and the alternatives were expensive.

Pasteurization, aside from killing *some* of the bacteria in the milk, destroys vitamins A, B, and C, enzymes, and calcium, and anything else in the milk that happens to be heat sensitive—including the lecithin which helps our bodies deal with the cholesterol of the fats.

Wherever it's available, children should be given *certified raw milk*—that is, milk which has been neither pasteurized nor homogenized (in homogenization the milk is forced through thin tubes against a hard surface, breaking up the fat molecules permanently, and giving the milk a shelf life of up to ten days), and which comes from certified herds. This means that local and federal health departments have inspected the cows, the procedures, and the workers, and found them free from disease—and certified them as such. Certified milk contains fewer bacteria than pasteurized milk. It's a fact.

And that is really *whole* milk.

Adults, conversely, should have nonfat milk.

There is a good deal of medical opinion around that American adults drink *too much* whole milk. Doctors have connected high milk consumption with kidney stones in adults. An old Viennese physician told us of an experiment interrupted by the *Anschluss* which indicated that adults who drank large amounts of milk had lower resistance to disease than adults who didn't. My husband stopped drinking whole milk from that day, and certainly his resistance has improved enormously.

Good skim milk is much easier to find than certified raw milk. Most health food stores carry non-instant, low-heat, spray-dried, nonfat milk. The low heat means that much of the goodness is still intact after processing. In the more widely distributed instant skim milks, the milk is dried by a high-heat process which leaves even less vitamin and mineral content than pasteurization.

So, for drinking, by all means try to get the low-heat, spray-dried, nonfat milk.

For baking, however, I use the instant, high-heat, nonfat milk, available in any supermarket. I use powdered milk because of the convenience. It measures so easily (I don't even have to reconstitute it, just pour it right into the bowl), and I never have to worry about warming it up out of the fridge (see Temperature of Ingredients, pp. 18–19).

Fats

So far as the *chemistry* of bread baking is concerned, all fats are interchangeable: oil or butter or margarine or hydrogenated shortenings or lard; for bread baking it makes no real difference. For your health, however, there is more than a little difference.*

You can't live without fats and oils. That's not an exaggeration. The fatty acids the body manufactures from the fats and oils you eat are absolutely vital to your life processes. But not all fats and oils are equally usable.

This brings us to saturated and unsaturated fats.

Think of fats as little charms. The body links these charms together into a charm bracelet called fatty acids. If the links of the charm are open and unattached, they can easily be linked up in these fatty acid chains. If the links are filled already (with hydrogen or oxygen), they cannot be formed into fatty acid chains. Those fats with open links are called unsaturated and are desirable. Those fats with filled links are called saturated and are undesirable.

Margarine is an example of a saturated fat. Most margarines start out as vegetable oils—naturally unsaturated, useful, wholesome. However, to make the margarine solid at room temperature, it is hydrogenated (that is, those once-open links are filled with hydrogen), which makes the fats saturated and undesirable. The situation with lard and "Crisco"-type shortenings is even worse: lard is so heavily "stabilized" today that it needn't even be refrigerated; and "Crisco"-type shortenings are hydrogenated and full of chemicals. (Also, read your margarine box; most margarines have chemicals too.)

There are several breads in this book made without any shortening at all. They are lower in calories than breads made with shortening, but are not of as smooth a texture and dry out faster.

When recipes call for shortening I use and recommend only unsaturated vegetable oils (corn, soy, safflower, etc.). Besides being healthier, vegetable oils are more convenient than hard shortening: they can be measured in the same cup as the honey, without cleaning, they never have to be creamed, and they blend quite easily with the flour.

In buying liquid oils, be careful about preservatives and other additives (some brands have as many as half

---

* While butter and margarine are about the same in terms of saturation, butter is the more desirable because of the chemicals in margarine.

a dozen chemical additives). Read the labels. Just because
an oil is liquid doesn't mean that it's wholesome.

Vegetable oils can be among our richest sources of
vitamin E (which the federal government has recently
conceded is necessary for good health). But the commercial hot-pressing process kills most of the vitamin E—
leaving us something unsaturated, but also vitaminless.
Baking also tends to kill much of the vitamin E. So, even
though we use any type of vegetable oil in our baking, we
make certain to use some *cold-pressed oil* every day (un-
heated, as in a salad dressing), to get some vitamin E.

Eggs

Eggs are a good food. They are fine protein and an excellent source of lecithin. (Did you stop eating eggs when
cholesterol became famous? Well, lecithin enables the
body to deal with the cholesterol the eggs contain.)

Have you been wondering why the shells on your
eggs are so much thinner than they used to be?

The last time you bought eggs directly from a farmer,
you may have noticed that not only were the shells
thicker but the eggs *tasted* better than supermarket eggs.

It's not your imagination. They have done something
to the eggs; or, rather, something to the chickens.

For, no doubt, sound economic reasons, the large-scale
chicken farmers from whom most of our eggs come do not
allow their chickens to run around and scratch for their
food. They are kept in chicken houses that get little day-
light or fresh air, and have never a bit of dirt to scratch
in. They get a supposedly balanced feed with just enough
minerals to produce an egg with just enough shell not to
break in transit, an egg that's nutritionally poorer than
the ones you had as a kid.

In order to lay a normal egg with a normal shell and
normal food values, a chicken has to be able to get out
in the sunshine and dirt and scratch around for its food.

That thin shell is symptomatic of what's wrong with
so many of our foods today. Chemical feeds and fertilizers are no substitute for good husbandry. Food taken
from heavily chemicaled soil and animals is poorer in
vitamins and minerals than food taken from plants and
animals grown organically.

Occasionally I have the opportunity to get organic eggs from a beekeeper. Not only are the shells thicker but the yolks are yellower, and the taste is vastly superior. I wish you the same opportunity.

In these recipes when I call for eggs, I mean large eggs. One size away—medium or extra large—will not make much difference, but if small eggs happen to be a good buy, substitute small eggs at the rate of three for two.

Salt

Does it seem to you that the salt has lost its savor? Well, in part it has. There are so many chemicals in the free-flowing salt that you buy in your neighborhood supermarket that there is, literally, less salt in the salt.

What is there instead?

Here's the label from the last box of supermarket salt I bought:

CONTAINS SALT
SODIUM SILICO ALUMINATE
DEXTROSE 0.1%
POTASSIUM IODIDE
YELLOW PRUSSIATE OF SODA
SODIUM BICARBONATE

And if that doesn't shake you, what does?

Salt, plus *five* chemicals (though iodine is necessary for health). I had one of my classes taste a bit of that salt and a bit of sea salt—and every student said that the sea salt was saltier. Those chemicals are there in large enough amounts to affect the saltiness of the salt, and you take them at every meal, every day.

You know, I hope, that federal law requires that packagers list ingredients in descending order by amount: that is, the ingredient there is most of comes first. If you'll look at that list again you'll see that "sodium silico aluminate" is listed second, and is therefore the second largest ingredient. I know of no use the body can make of aluminum at all!

What are your options? If you don't want sodium silico aluminate and yellow prussiate of soda and so forth, what can you do?

Our solution has been to switch to sea salt.

Sea salt is evaporated from seawater and comes

either as (relatively) pure sodium chloride (with traces of sea minerals quite vital to life) or as sodium chloride with magnesium carbonate added (both are naturally iodized).

Eating magnesium carbonate is okay because magnesium is needed by the body to help absorb calcium* and most of us—except for those living in Deaf Smith County, Texas, where the high magnesium level of the soil prevents tooth decay and bone fractures—have chronic magnesium deficiencies from eating food grown on chemical fertilizers.

Another option you have is to switch, at least in part, from salt to granulated kelp. Kelp is seaweed, and ground and dried kelp is nutritious and quite tasty—and a little salty as well as particularly high in iodine and calcium. I keep it in a shaker and use it on eggs and meat and any other food where I once used salt.

(Kosher salt, a *coarse* salt good for sprinkling on top of baking breads or pretzels, has only one chemical—polysorbate 80, whatever that is. It is used for the koshering of meats and poultry—that is, the rubbing down of the steak, for instance, to absorb and eliminate blood.)

All the recipes in this book were standardized to the tastes of my students, using saltier salt—sea salt. If you're using four- or five-chemical supermarket salt, you may want to slightly increase the amount called for. Whatever salt you use, don't hesitate to change the amount if it doesn't suit your taste.

Salt has a role in baking aside from bringing out flavors: because salt, in goodly amounts, will destroy microorganisms (including yeast), it functions as a stabilizer in retarding yeast growth.

So there it is: my white flour is unbleached enriched white; my whole grains are stone ground; my milk is powdered skim milk; I use only honey or blackstrap molasses for sweetener; my salt may be saltier than yours; my oil is only vegetable oil, unsaturated and unpreserved; and my yeast is active dry yeast.

* For those of you who want to know more about such things as why magnesium and calcium have to balance, and what a complete protein is, and which vitamins you are likely to be deficient in, I suggest you read Adelle Davis's *Let's Eat Right to Keep Fit*, available in paper from Signet Books.

SOME GENERAL PROCEDURES

The different kinds of breads we'll bake, though all of
them yeast breads, have similarities and differences in
preparation. The differences will be described in the specific chapters, but here, for easy reference, is a list of
some procedures used in making almost any bread.

At the end of the procedures to *do,* you'll find a short
list of procedures to *don't.* I would suggest you read that
—it may surprise you.

Measurements

I don't own a measuring spoon. You don't need one either,
not to bake the breads in this book. A teaspoon or a tablespoon will do equally well. I must admit that I do use a
measuring cup—but you don't have to. You could use a
teacup for your measuring, and so long as you used the
same cup for liquid and flour, the proportions would be
correct and the bread would come out fine.

As for whether the cups are level or heaped, packed
or loose, it hardly matters. There is no absolute amount
of flour, even if you repeat the same bread day after day.
The amount of flour will vary according to humidity and
temperature, when, where, and how the strain of wheat
was grown, and according to how muscular you feel. So
any of my recipes that call for a specific amount of flour
should have the word "about" in parentheses.

Baking is not an exact science, and those who say
"exactly . . ." are kidding you or themselves. Baking deals
with physical changes that take place within a very broad
range—a broad range of temperatures, and a broad range
of chemical proportions.

Temperature of Ingredients

More battles for happy bread baking are won or lost on
this battlefield than any other. When we discussed active
dry yeast, I told you that it was much more heat resistant
than the old cake yeast, and could be stimulated to faster
growth by higher temperatures. That's not just an interesting fact. It is a key.

I got a call from a student one day (all my students

get permanent consultation privileges) complaining that a Challah refused to rise. After some questioning (Nero Wolf and I never leave our homes to solve a case) I found that she had used milk from the refrigerator. I reminded her that in class we had used *hot* water to make up the Challah. "But I let it come to room temperature!" Room temperature for that day was about 70°—roughly *half* the temperature of the water we had used in class. I told her to give the bread more time and to put it in a warmer place. The Challah eventually rose, and she finally had a successful bread.

So, if you change any of my water recipes to milk, or any cold liquid, heat it—certainly not to boiling, but to the temperature of hot tap water.

Eggs should be at room temperature. If you forget to take them out of the fridge beforehand, put them in a bowl of hot tap water for a few minutes and the temperature will be fine.

Oil should be at room temperature if you are using more than a few tablespoons.

Any cold—or even *cool*—ingredient will slow down the yeast.

That doesn't mean that you are to heat up everything to boiling. If you must heat an ingredient on the stove, stick a finger in to make sure the temperature is bearable. If it doesn't burn you it won't kill the yeast.

All this is especially true when you deal with my New Method Breads. They just won't work if you use cool ingredients.

Rising Dough

Yeast breads rise. The yeast plants make bubbles of carbon dioxide and the elastic gluten expands like balloons filling. Then, in the baking, after the yeast has been killed off, the heat expands the air bubbles further and you get more rise. Some breads rise just in the bowl, like Nan. Some breads rise just in the pan, like Method Breads. Most breads rise both in the bowl and as loaves, like 100 Percent Whole Wheat Bread or Brioches.

If left to their own devices, the yeast plants would make carbon dioxide at a leisurely pace—or, if your kitchen is cool, a quite slow pace. To encourage the yeast to work faster, the dough should be put in a very warm place. For me, the pilot light on my gas range is that place. (For a country friend, a large warm rock out in the summer sun is that place.) I put the bowl of dough on a trivet, cover the bowl, and there the yeast, stimulated by the heat, gases away at a satisfactory rate. So much for dough in the bowl. But what about dough after it has been shaped into loaves? That pilot just isn't big enough for three loaves of whole wheat bread, or two huge Challah. What then? If it's winter there's no difficulty. I put a piece of fieldstone on my kitchen radiator, and put the covered loaves on the stone.

But what about the warmer weather? Here's where you have to be inventive. I rise by hot water, and here's how.

Loaves in pans (especially New Method Breads). I make certain the water is good and hot, and then I run a few inches of water into my sink or bathtub (that's right—I said bathtub). I stand or float the pans of dough in this hot water, and then I take a towel and tent over the sink. (If your bathtub is deep, you needn't tent it over —just make sure the windows and doors are shut against drafts.) Breads will rise in their pans very quickly this way because the warmth surrounds them.

Free-standing loaves on baking sheets. Most baking sheets are too shallow to stand directly in water, so what I do is run the same few inches of water into the sink or bathtub, and invert heavy cups or some similar objects for the baking sheets to balance on—just out of the water. I then tent over as before.

Don't panic if a little water gets onto a loaf or into a pan: just pour it off. I have seen completely drowned loaves bake up very satisfactorily.

You can also rise on the top of the stove—if, like mine, yours gets very hot on the work surface. I light my stove and put my covered loaves on top, then shut the oven off after 15 minutes. Of course, that isn't practical if the particular type of bread you are baking must go into a cold oven. Free-standing loaves risen this way (or by any intense bottom heat) have a tendency to rise *wide* instead of *high.*

Dough can be risen out of the kitchen—on the back of a television set, radio, or hi-fi (but not solid state sets;

they don't generate the heat), or on top of an old-fashioned refrigerator.

If none of these works for you, figure out your own method.

Order of Ingredients

There is nothing sacred about my order of ingredients. I've found it quick and simple, but there is no need to follow it if you prefer some other. Of course, if you decide to put the flour in first or the yeast last, you might have some difficult experiences.

Greasing

You have to grease your loaf pans, casseroles, baking sheets, and so forth, or your breads won't come out. I grease with melted margarine or butter—*not oil*. The vegetable oils (which I use exclusively within the recipes) are polyunsaturated—they have small molecules. The hardened fats, like butter and margarine, are saturated and have *large* molecules. These large molecules make for better greasing because they don't absorb as readily into the bread. This means that more of the grease stays on the pan or baking sheet. Oil's small molecules get absorbed into the bread, which means poor lubrication (and more sticking), and that you actually consume more of the grease.

I brush on the melted margarine with a pastry brush, and find this method very satisfactory. But, if you prefer, you can rub directly with the stick (though this often leaves ungreased spots), or with greased fingers, or with the greasy butter wrapper.

Tests for Doneness

I test for doneness with a thin clean knife, a cake tester (a piece of wire the length of a broom straw), or, occasionally, a toothpick, and here's how I do it.

First of all, turn the bread out of its pan. (This turning out means gripping the rim of the pan with a potholder and turning it upside down onto a clean towel held in your free hand or spread out on some surface. If the bread is stubborn and sticks, work a thin knife around the edges of the pan, then try again.) I turn my breads out (with a few exceptions) so as to test through the bottom of the loaf. You could test through the top, but testing through the bottom leaves the top unscarred, and there's something very satisfying about that "perfect" loaf brought to the table.

Now that you have your turned-out loaf, stick a thin, clean (the *clean* is important—dough sticks to anything) knife or cake tester through the palest part of the bottom, all the way *almost to the top*. If there is any unbaked dough, it will most likely be near the top, so you have to go all the way in. Give the knife or tester a little wiggle from side to side (to enlarge the hole slightly), draw it out, and really give it a squint. You have to distinguish between unbaked dough—which comes out in lumps and if allowed to stay on the knife will harden—and water vapor, which wipes right off. Water vapor is fine, but any unbaked dough means that the loaf must go back to the oven.

I use a toothpick on breads like Brioches and Challah and Method Sally Lunn—and I test these breads through the top. The Challah gets tested at a juncture of a center braid, a Brioche gets tested right at the neck, and Sally Lunn gets hers through any pale place on top (Sally is glazed during baking, and you can't turn her out).

Bottom color can be an indication of doneness, if you know what it should look like. Though I prefer to think of it as a *clue* to when to test.

Thumping is sometimes recommended. You take the turned-out loaf in one hand and thump the bottom with the other. A hollow sound is supposed to say "done." It works sometimes. But sometimes it leaves you with a lovely hollow of undone dough in the middle.

So, for me, knife or cake-tester testing is the only sure way. *And you must test.* There is nothing so disappointing as bringing a lovely-looking loaf to the table and cutting in to find so much mush.

There are few detection devices as good as your nose for telling when a loaf is *approaching* doneness. For as it bakes, the aroma of baking gets quite strong. Even if you think the bread can't possibly be done yet—if it begins to smell good, check it. It may be that a hot spot is scorching one loaf and you'll want to turn it, or the bread may be done. So, if you can smell it—take a look.

Glazes

Glazes are put on a bread to change the taste, color, or texture of the crust, or (most important) to hold on seeds or whatever you sprinkle over the top.

Melted butter or margarine glazes. These should be brushed on when the loaf is removed from the oven and are put on a loaf to give it a shinier look. If you put them on early in the baking, they will give you a browner top, but no shine.

Egg glazes. These can be put on at any time up to the last few minutes of baking (they do require a few minutes of cooking on the loaf) and still come out beautiful. Just smear the egg (yolk or white or whole, according to the recipe) over the surface with your fingers or a pastry brush. An egg glaze can make a loaf look done before its time. Don't be fooled.

Honey-and-fruit-juice glaze. This glaze should be spooned over the loaf as soon as it's out of the oven.

Milk glaze. This glaze will give a browner crust to pale breads and rolls; it gets brushed on at the beginning, and can have the effect of softening your crust.

If you forget to put a glaze on at the beginning, don't worry—the middle of the baking will do, too.

If you forget to glaze as soon as the loaf comes out of the oven, don't worry—you can put it on 10 minutes later and still get a shiny effect.

Whisk Cleaning

I like to use a wire whisk to beat the batter in the early stages of mixing. Not that a spoon doesn't do the job— a whisk does it faster. But a whisk (or the beaters of your electric mixer) can be a cleaning problem, with all the batter sticking. Here's what to do. Keep some of the flour to be used handy in a measuring cup. When you want to switch from whisk (or beaters) to spoon or hand, dip the whisk into the flour and wipe everything off into the mixing bowl. The batter and flour wipe off easily and completely.

Pans

You don't have to own every size pan, casserole, and ring mold called for in these recipes. Any recipe for a ring mold will go into small pans, too. But you should be aware that the volume of a pan goes up enormously with only a little change in the dimensions: a pan $8\frac{1}{2}'' \times 4\frac{1}{2}'' \times 2\frac{1}{2}''$ holds 50 percent more than a pan $8'' \times 4'' \times 2''$. So, don't move to another size pan without changing the number of pans. If you don't have two large pans, three small pans will do.

Cooling on a Wire Rack

As a loaf of bread fresh from the oven cools, it gives off water vapor. The vapor from the sides and top goes off into the air. Fine. The vapor from the bottom will also go into the air *if the loaf sits on a wire rack*. If the loaf sits on a dish, table, board, or any similar surface, the condensing water will absorb back into the loaf, making the bottom a little soggy, instead of crisp as it should be. Observe your first loaf on the rack. You'll see the water drops on the surface below—a good reason for keeping the rack off any surface likely to water-stain.

DON'T

Don't Sift Flour. You would sift only if you were afraid of lumps or you wanted an exact measurement. No commercially packaged flour is lumpy today, and in bread baking you don't care about exact measurements. So don't make extra work for yourself. Worse yet, if you were to sift whole-grain flours you could be discarding some of the healthiest parts.

Don't "Pre-soften" Yeast. The only yeast I recommend in this book (apart from grow-it-yourself sourdough) is active dry yeast. Only cake yeast needs to be presoftened or proved or made into a sponge—which I won't explain here because you don't need to know it. Active dry yeast goes right into the bowl, dry. If you dissolve it in water first, you're wasting time and effort, and will only give yourself an additional dish to wash. I hate washing dishes—which is one reason most of the recipes in this book are one-bowl recipes.

Don't Break Eggs into a Separate Bowl. That's a hangover from the good old days when the chances were that in any dozen eggs you'd find one that was bad. It's been fifteen years since I've had a bad egg. Again, it's just extra work and extra dishes.

Don't Scald Milk. Unless you bake with raw milk, don't scald milk. Scalding was done to destroy certain milk enzymes that retarded yeast growth. The milk was heated to just below boiling, and then cooled to room temperature. Pasteurization gets rid of most of those same enzymes, if you insist on using whole milk. But I do strongly recommend powdered milk instead. It's much easier.

Don't Preheat Oven. Unless the recipe specifically says so, don't preheat. The baking times I give (and God knows they'll be different for your oven anyhow) are, except for those recipes that call for preheating, for cold ovens—that is. starting *below* 200°.

☞ 2 ☜

New
Method
Breads

*Though this be madness, yet
there is method in't.*

Color it 5 P.M. Color dinner for 6:30. Color yourself with
the sudden desire for fresh bread with dinner. What can
you have? Brown-and-serve rolls? Something from the
bakery? Baking powder biscuits?

No! You can have fresh, homemade, steaming-from-
the-oven yeast bread, made on the spot by you *in an hour
and a half or less*, without kneading, without special equipment, without special skill—and without preservatives or
chemical additives. You can have New Method Breads,
*and still have plenty of time to cook the rest of dinner,
even if you've never baked before!* These breads are so
simple it's hard to believe.

I discovered this method by mistake, in one of my
baking classes.

The class was running late and a Cheese Batter Bread
was last on the agenda. After the batter was beaten (I
was watching the testing of a Pumpernickel that refused
to get done), a student poured the batter directly into
greased pans instead of setting it in a bowl to rise. (This
rising in the bowl is a procedure common to all Batter
Breads and Kneaded Breads.) I "rescued" the batter and
put it to rise for the prescribed hour ("then punch down
and rise for 30 minutes . . ."). Well, as I'd feared, the
session broke up before the bread was baked, and everyone left with a complete disinterest in Batter Breads.
After all—this was a class with three weeks experience

in Kneaded Breads. They enjoyed kneading, were good at it, and found it satisfying. If a bread was going to take that long—they'd rather do a Kneaded Bread, thank you very much.

Later, I got to wondering what would have happened if I hadn't fixed that mistake. In fact, why should I rise the batter at all?

And the only reason was that recipes for batter breads say so.

Well, that wasn't reason enough. Recipes tell you to do all kinds of things you don't have to do.

So, I tried a batch and didn't rise the batter in the bowl at all. Just as that student had done accidentally, I turned the batter into baking pans as soon as I'd beaten it, then gave it just a 20-minute rise in the pans. And the result was a Cheese Method Bread, completed in less than 1½ hours—the time it originally took just to rise the batter bread.

Kneaded Breads, Batter Breads, and New Method Breads—just what are the differences?

Every bread starts with a "batter"; that's the sticky glop in your bowl when you've mixed in all the ingredients except, perhaps, the last bit of flour.

If you add that last flour and knead it on a board, then shape the dough, you have Kneaded Bread—and, believe me, there's nothing in the world like Kneaded Bread for evenness of texture and "picture-perfect" loaves.

If, to return to that sticky glop in your bowl, you didn't add that last bit of flour, but beat the batter, and let it rise once, twice, even three times for from 1½ to 3 hours—you have Batter Breads—very good, especially if you can't—or won't—knead.

If you beat the batter and then pour it directly into a greased baking pan to rise for 20 minutes, and then bake it, you have New Method Breads: every bit as good as Batter Breads that take three times as long to prepare, and without the work of Kneaded Breads.

Don't mistake me, these are not no-work breads. These are yeast breads, and all yeast breads must be worked somewhat to develop the gluten—the protein part of the flour that makes it elastic or rubbery when you handle it. This elasticity holds the air bubbles formed by

the yeast and allows yeast breads to rise. Either beating
or kneading will develop the gluten. Both are work.
Kneaded Breads must be worked for anywhere from 10 to
20 minutes—Method Breads are *beaten* a total of 4 to 6
minutes.

In the next chapter we'll take up kneading, but now,
even before you've kneaded a single bit of dough, you
can follow these four quick and easy steps that take you
from a great idea to a delicious light yeast bread:

1. Mix and beat the ingredients in one bowl with
one spoon.
2. Dump this resulting batter into greased baking
pans immediately.
3. Leave these pans in a warm place to rise for only
20 minutes. (This allows rising action to begin—rising will
finish during the next step.)
4. Put them in a cold oven and bake.

Details of what you'll see during the baking (yes, you
can open the oven during baking without collapses) ac-
company the individual recipes. Here are a few general
hints.

GENERAL HINTS

☞ In all the recipes, you'll notice that I call for
vigorous beating of the batter *before* all the flour is in.
The why is very simple; it's much easier to beat a thin
mixture with 3 cups of flour than a heavy, almost solid
mixture with 4½. The gluten is developed in the thinner
batter, and it does save muscle power.

To save even more muscle, you might want to use an
electric mixer for this part of the work. There's no real
time saving. You substitute 1 minute of electric beating
at a medium speed for 3 minutes of hand beating, but
then you have to clean the beaters. (Dip them in some of
the remaining flour and rub the batter off with your
fingers.)

☞ Fill your pans *less than half full* of the batter.
Unless it is a very small pan, filling more than halfway
leads to possible sagging and, in any case, to an increase
in baking time.

☞ All these recipes for New Method Breads make (as you might guess) New Method Rolls. Use a muffin tray—or trays—greasing them and filling each mold with a ball or lump of dough a little more than halfway (yes, that's okay for rolls—they never sag), and bake for about 25 minutes in a slow (325°) oven.

☞ Do not preheat your oven. It is basic to Method Breads that they start in a cold oven; in this way the yeast is given a last chance to grow before baking kills it off. However, the dough continues to rise even after the yeast is dead—the heat expands the bubbles that have already been made.

If you have been using your oven before you begin your bread making, shut it off for a while and leave the door open; bring the temperature down below 200° before you put in your bread and relight.

HERB METHOD BREAD

If there is a basic Method Bread, this is it. We give the recipe here as an Herb Bread, but: if you omit the herbs, you have plain White Method Bread; if you substitute whole wheat flour for some of the white, you have Tan Method Bread; juggle the herbs, spices, and flavorings and you have a sweeter or spicier loaf.

The web (the arrangement of holes you see in the slice of bread) has a coarse, homemade look that is most satisfying, and the loaf has a rough texture unlike any packaged or bakery bread.

Since it cuts well (even slicing thin when cool), it is good for making hearty sandwiches. Or, hot, tear it apart as you would a Garlic Bread.

Hot or cooled, sliced or torn, this one is an exciting introduction to Method Breads.

HERB METHOD BREAD

For the Batter:
    2 tbsp. active dry yeast
    1 tsp. dill seed
    1 tsp. savory
    ½ tsp. dill weed
    1 tbsp. sea salt
    2 tbsp. honey
    2 cups hot water
    ⅔ cup skim milk powder
    4½ cups unbleached white flour
For Greasing:
    butter or margarine
Equipment:
    mixing bowl, mixing spoon, 2 loaf pans 8½″ × 4½″ ×
    2½″ (also, if you like, wire whisk and rubber spatula)

Mixing

Measure the **yeast** (2 tablespoons of yeast is the same as 2 packages of yeast is the same as ½ ounce of yeast), **herbs, salt, honey, hot water,** and **skim milk powder** into one large bowl and stir with a spoon or wire whisk until the honey is dissolved. (The mixture will look quite strange—a murky white with flecks of green herbs appearing and disappearing.)

Add the **first 3 cups of flour,** a cup at a time, stirring gently until you have wetted the flour; the flour will fly all over the kitchen if beaten energetically while still dry.

When you have the 3 cups of flour all wet, beat the resulting batter *vigorously* for about 3 minutes, or beat it *lazily* for 5 minutes (or with an electric beater at medium speed for 1 minute). It's the number of movements that counts, not the violence. You don't have to exhaust yourself to make good bread. Remember, we beat now to save some hard work later.

Add the **next cup of flour,** about ¼ cup at a time, and beat for another minute or so, even though it's harder now. If you've been using a wire whisk, you'll want to shift at this point to a spoon. If you find the batter too stiff to beat with a spoon, work it with your bare hand for a couple of minutes, squeezing the batter through your fingers. Don't be afraid to touch it; getting sticky can be fun.

Work in the **last ⅓ cup of flour** well.

(The dough is ready when, as you pull the spoon or your hand from the batter, the mixture forms into rubbery sheets.)

Filling the Pans

Grease well two baking pans 8½″ × 4½″ × 2½″ (don't get thrown by the figures—that's a standard size). Don't forget to grease the top rim, we want the loaves to turn out of the pans easily.

Dump half the batter into each pan, dividing as equally as you can.

It's not easy to get the batter out of the mixing bowl and divided—it's very cohesive now and still sticky, and has to be helped out of the bowl and then poked into the corners of the pans. Corners that aren't filled now stay unfilled, making air pockets. I find the back of a greased spoon (or just a bare greased hand) handy for poking into unfilled corners and for smoothing out the top of the loaf. You can't make the top perfectly smooth; a rough top is one of the marks of this kind of bread.

Unless you are using very small pans, fill your pans *less than half full.* If you have too much batter for your two pans, grease a muffin pan and use the excess to make some Method Rolls.

Resting the Batter

Once the batter is turned into the pans, cover them with a clean towel and put them in a very warm place for 20 minutes (see Rising, pp. 19–21).

Baking

After 20 minutes—the batter has risen slightly—put the pans into a *cold oven* and light a low flame. (If your oven has a thermostat, set for 200°–250° for the first 10 minutes, and then raise to 350°–375°.)

Bake for about 50 minutes, total.

If, like mine, your oven has hot spots, look at the loaves after about 20 minutes and, if they are browner on one side, rotate them.

When done, the tops of the loaves should have an even, chocolate-brown color and the bottoms and sides should be golden brown.

Turn the loaves out and test for doneness (see pp. 21–23).

When finished, cool the loaves on a wire rack or bring them right to the table steaming hot, and tear apart or cut gently with a serrated knife. (They are easier to cut when cooled, but taste better when hot.)

Options

☞ As soon as the loaves are removed from the oven and turned out, brush the tops with **melted butter or margarine** for a shiny, happier look.

☞ If you're baking for children, use **2 cups of whole milk** instead of the water and skim milk powder. Richer yet, use whole milk *and* milk powder. (See pp. 12–13.)

☞ To make Tan Method Bread, substitute **2 cups of whole wheat flour** and **2 cups of white flour** for the 4½ cups of white in the recipe. That ½ cup is left out because whole wheat flour absorbs more water than white.

☞ Another excellent herb combination is **1 teaspoon basil, 1 teaspoon oregano,** and **½ teaspoon tarragon.** Or **caraway** can be substituted happily for the dill seeds.

☞ You can substitute **celery salt, garlic salt, dill salt,** or any **seasoned salt** to your liking for half the salt in the recipe.

☞ **Half a teaspoon of fresh-ground pepper** added to your favorite herb batter makes a delightful Pepper Herb Bread.

☞ Try any combination, using between 2 and 3 teaspoons of your favorite herbs: only you know what you like.

☞ Add **2 tablespoons of any unsaturated vegetable oil** to the recipe to improve its keeping power—though, in our house, keeping this bread is never a problem: it's always eaten within two days.

☞ Substitute **½ cup of wheat germ** for the last ½ cup of flour.

HERB METHOD BREAD—SUMMARY

A. 2 tbsp. active dry yeast   B. 4½ cups flour
   1 tsp. dill seed
   1 tsp. savory
   ½ tsp. dill weed
   1 tbsp. sea salt
   2 tbsp. honey
   2 cups hot water
   ⅔ cup skim milk powder

Measure A into a large mixing bowl and stir.

Add 3 cups of B, 1 cup at a time, and beat vigorously for 3 minutes by hand (1 minute by electric beater).

Add fourth cup of B, ½ cup at a time, and beat for another minute or so.

Work last ½ cup of B in well.

Grease two 8½″ × 4½″ × 2½″ loaf pans.

Scrape in the batter, poke it into all the corners, smooth the top with greased fingers or spatula.

Rise in hot water or in a warm place, covered, for 20 minutes.

Bake for 10 minutes at 200°–250°, then for 40 minutes at 350°–375°.

Knife-test for doneness.

Cool on a wire rack and eat hot.

PEANUT METHOD BREAD

This may be the world's fastest bread. The last loaf I baked took me just one hour and five minutes from start to finish, not including the time it takes to shell enough peanuts for half a cup. I recommend my no-work method for shelling—I get my husband to do it. (Since all nuts keep best in the shell, don't shell them too long before your baking.)

I grind the nuts right into the mixing bowl with a Mouli grater—really excellent for this—leaving whatever chunks leap out of the grater right there in the bowl.

To save time, you can use a half cup of peanut butter. In some stores you can buy fresh, ground-while-you-wait peanut butter—much healthier than the homogenized commercial kinds whose oils are hardened to keep longer

on the shelf. The healthier fresh-ground kind is not homogenized: it doesn't keep as long (all healthly oils have
a relatively short life and require refrigeration), but is
much better for you and your children.

If you use salted nuts—the last resort—reduce the
salt in the recipe by a half teaspoon. (The salt doesn't so
much keep the nuts from going rancid as it keeps you
from tasting the slight rancidity of the peanut oil.)

Peanut Method Bread is best finished by hand. Beat
in the first 2½ cups of flour by spoon, whisk, or electric
beater; then work in the last ½ cup of flour by squeezing
the batter between your fingers; then continue by hand
for an additional 2 minutes. This is quite a dry batter, and
it will divide easily and go into the baking cans without
trouble.

You'll see in the recipe that this is a tan bread—half
whole wheat and half unbleached white flour. This, together with the peanuts (which are high in protein), makes
it an ideal bread for children: it's healthy, and the coffee-
can shape of the loaves makes attractive—and different
—round sandwiches.

If you've got a problem eater, this bread may be a
partial solution, especially if you use the dough scraped
off your hand to make his initial on the top of the loaf.
The scrapings are enough for one fat initial.

PEANUT METHOD BREAD

For Batter:
   2 tbsp. active dry yeast
   ¼ cup honey
   2 tsp. sea salt
   1¼ cups hot water
   ½ cup shelled peanuts
   1½ cups whole wheat flour
   1½ cups unbleached white flour
For Greasing:
   butter or margarine
Equipment:
   large bowl, mixing spoon, two 1-pound coffee cans

Mixing

Measure the yeast, honey, salt, and water into a large
mixing bowl and stir well, dissolving the honey.

Grate in ½ cup of shelled, roasted peanuts. Stir.

Add **1 cup of whole wheat flour,** and mix in.

Add **1 cup of white flour,** and mix in.

When the flours are thoroughly wet, beat vigorously by hand for 2 minutes, or moderately for 3 minutes (or by electric mixer for 1 minute).

Add the **last ½ cup of whole wheat flour** and stir.

Add the **last ½ cup of white flour** and work in by hand (one hand is enough), squeezing the dough and turning it to get in all the flour.

Continue to work by hand for another 2 minutes.

Filling the Cans

Grease well two 1-pound coffee cans. It is especially important to grease coffee cans generously because the ridges tend to hold the bread in.

Divide the batter in half and put half into each coffee can—filling less than half full: below the second ridge of a 3-ridge can.

The claylike dough you scrape from your hand is enough to make an initial (or design) on top of one loaf. By now the dough will roll easily between your palms.

Resting the Batter

Cover the cans with a clean towel and put into a very warm place to rise for 20 minutes.

There will be *little* evidence of rising: don't panic.

Baking

Put into a cold oven, set at medium (about 375°), and bake for 30–35 minutes.

If you peek after 10 minutes, you'll see some rising. In all, the dough about doubles before it's finished.

One sign of approaching doneness is a browning of the top. (Don't forget that this is a tan bread to begin with.) If after 30 minutes the top hasn't begun to brown —let it go for a while longer.

When the top has begun to brown, turn a loaf out of its coffee can and test through the bottom for doneness (see pp. 22–23). When the loaf is done, the sides and bottom have a dark, golden brown look.

If you've made an initial or design on the top, it will stand out beautifully because it bakes darker than the rest of the top.

Cool the loaves on a wire rack or eat them hot.

This bread slices beautifully, and has an even, fine web—honey won't drip through.

Options

☞ If your family really loves peanuts, use **more nuts** in the recipe and include more unground nuts.

☞ You might try another nut altogether—say, **filberts** or **walnuts.**

☞ If you use a 1½-quart casserole you'll get an even crisper crust because the thick sides of the casserole hold the heat. In this case, you'll have enough dough left over for a couple of rolls. The casserole takes 20 minutes longer to bake: 45–50 minutes at the same temperature. The rolls (dropped onto a greased cookie sheet or muffin pan) should be ready in less than 25 minutes.

☞ For an even higher-protein and lower-starch bread, substitute gluten flour for the white flour (see Gluten Flour, p. 5). If you do, double the salt in the recipe.

PEANUT METHOD BREAD—SUMMARY

A. 2 tbsp. active dry   B. ½ cup shelled peanuts
    yeast
    ¼ cup honey   C. 1½ cups whole wheat flour
    2 tsp. sea salt
    1¼ cups hot water   D. 1½ cups white flour

Measure A into a large bowl and stir.

Grate in B.

Mix in 1 cup of C.

Mix in 1 cup of D. Beat vigorously for 2 minutes by hand (1 minute by mixer).

Stir in last ½ cup of C.

Work in last ¼ cup of D by hand, then work for 2 more minutes.

Grease well two 1-pound coffee cans.

Divide batter in half and dump into the two cans, poking batter into the corners and smoothing the tops.

(An initial or design can be made from the dough scraped off your hand.)

Rise for 20 minutes in a warm place.

Put into a cold oven and bake at medium (375°) for 30–35 minutes.

Knife-test for doneness.

Cool on a wire rack, or eat warm.

DARK WHOLE WHEAT RAISIN METHOD BREAD

Bring on the kiddies! or anyone else who has trouble keeping a balanced diet. This bread is so healthy it's hard to believe it can taste as good as it does.

This is a very dark whole wheat bread—the blackstrap molasses helps make it so. Don't be put off by blackstrap—there's no bitterness by the time you've finished baking, and this very dark molasses is rich in iron and minerals. The raisins add to the iron and food energy, the eggs provide protein, and the whole wheat flour provides those B-complex vitamins that disappear in the milling of white flour.

This recipe makes two loaves—ideal for sandwiches, or toast, or whatever you like.

I strongly recommend rising this one by sitting the baking pans in very hot tap water and tenting them with a towel. Whole wheat flour is heavier than white (in the textural sense), and the hot water which almost surrounds your pan stimulates the rising better than any "warm place."

The batter, though wet, is easy to handle, but it does need a greased spoon to poke it into the corners of the pan.

Much as I hate to mention it, there is a drawback to this very healthful bread: since there is no honey to retard spoilage, Dark Whole Wheat Raisin Method Bread will start to get moldy within a few days. So, if you are a family of one or two, freeze one loaf after baking.

DARK WHOLE WHEAT RAISIN METHOD BREAD

For Batter:
  2 tbsp. active dry yeast
  ¼ cup blackstrap molasses
  1 tbsp. sea salt
  2 cups hot water
  ⅔ cup skim milk powder
  2 tbsp. vegetable oil
  2 large eggs (at room temperature)
  4½ cups whole wheat flour
  1 cup raisins
For Greasing:
  butter or margarine
Equipment:
  mixing bowl, spoon (wire whisk is optional), 2 loaf
  pans 8½″ × 4½″ × 2½″

Mixing

Into the mixing bowl measure the **yeast, molasses, salt, hot water,** and **skim milk powder,** and stir well, dissolving the molasses.

Mix in the **oil.**

Break the **eggs** into the bowl and beat the mixture with a spoon or wire whisk until the eggs are mixed in.

Add **2 cups of the flour,** and stir well until smooth.

Add **1 cup of flour** and, when worked in, stir briskly for 3 minutes (or beat by electric beater for 1 minute). You are allowed to rest if your arm is weary: the gluten doesn't mind.

Stir in the **raisins,** making sure that they are well worked into the mixture. Every bit of handling you give the batter is to the good, so don't skimp.

Add the **fourth cup of flour,** and when this is worked in, beat for 1 minute.

If you've been using a whisk, at this point you'll want to switch over to a spoon. Work in the last ½ cup of flour and your batter is ready.

Filling the Pans

Grease two 8½-inch loaf pans.

Scrape the bits of batter off the sides of your mixing bowl and onto the main lump. Then, with your spoon or with a knife, cut through the batter, dividing it in half. Spoon each half into a pan, being certain that the pans are filled no more than halfway. (Again, if there is a little excess, you can make a couple of Method Rolls. See p. 29.)

With your fingers or a greased spoon (you can grease the same spoon you've been using all along) poke the batter into the corners. Also, smooth off the top of the loaf as well as you can without making it your life work.

Rising

Rise these pans of batter in hot water (see p. 20), covered, for 20 minutes.

You will see some rising begin.

Baking

Put the loaves into a cold oven, light, and set the flame at low (200°) for the first 10 minutes, then raise to medium (375°) thereafter.

After 10 minutes the loaves will have risen to the tops of their pans.

After 20 minutes you will see a loaf shape and more rising.

The loaves should be done in 35–40 minutes. The tops will be dark, but don't judge by color—test.

Turn the loaves out onto a wire rack and cool.

Options

☞ You can substitute **honey** for any or all of the molasses if you prefer a sweeter bread and one lighter in color. But, believe me, it's worthwhile trying this recipe with molasses before you decide to switch.

☞ The butterfat level of the bread can be raised by substituting **whole milk** for the hot water and milk powder. But don't forget to warm the milk—the yeast doesn't like it cold.

☞ You can glaze the loaves, when they come out of the oven, with a slathering of **melted butter or margarine** brushed over the top.

DARK WHOLE WHEAT RAISIN
METHOD BREAD—SUMMARY

A. 2 tbsp. active dry yeast
  $\frac{1}{4}$ cup blackstrap molasses
  1 tbsp. sea salt
  2 cups hot water
  $\frac{2}{3}$ cup skim milk powder

B. 2 tbsp. vegetable oil
  2 large eggs

C. $4\frac{1}{2}$ cups whole wheat
  flour

D. 1 cup raisins

Measure A into a large mixing bowl, and stir.

Add B, and beat until the eggs are mixed in.

Add 2 cups of C and stir well until smooth.

Add another cup of C and beat briskly for 3 minutes by hand (1 minute by mixer).

Stir in D, distributing uniformly.

Add a fourth cup of C, then beat for 1 minute.

Work in the last $\frac{1}{2}$ cup of C.

Grease two $8\frac{1}{2}$-inch loaf pans.

Scrape half the batter into each pan. Poke the batter into any corners, and smooth the surface with a greased hand or spatula.

Set to rise in hot water for 20 minutes.

Bake at 200° for the first 10 minutes, then 375° for 25–30 minutes.

Knife-test for doneness.

Cool on a wire rack, and serve warm.

CHEESE METHOD BREAD

This is the one that started it all—the first Method Bread ever made. And a succulent beginning it is.

It's excellent for sandwiches (hot open sandwiches with gravy, too). It is also marvelous hot from the oven, torn rather than cut. A casserole loaf of Cheese Method Bread has a crispy side and bottom crust that doesn't need butter or any other spread. It's a good keeper, as the cheese helps to hold moisture.

Use Cheddar cheése, sharp or mild, weighing out (or buying) 6 ounces of it beforehand, then cutting it into grater-sized chunks so you can grate it right into the bowl. And do keep the cheese cold until you're ready to use it. If you let the cheese come to room temperature, it won't grate.

Cheese Method Bread makes up into a wet-looking batter. In fact, the batter stays so relatively thin that it's possible to use a wire whisk throughout. When you're ready to dump the batter into the coffee cans and/or casseroles, you merely spoon the mixture in.

But this doesn't mean that the batter is not elastic. It is. It will show that rubbery-sheeting look when you dip out the spoonfuls. If it doesn't, beat it some more.

CHEESE METHOD BREAD

For Batter:
    2 tbsp. active dry yeast
    3 tbsp. honey
    1 tbsp. sea salt
    2 cups hot water
    ⅔ cup skim milk powder
    2 tbsp. vegetable oil
    2 cups unbleached white flour (more to come)
    1 large egg
    6 oz. cheese (grates to 2 cups)
    3 more cups unbleached white flour
For Greasing:
    butter or margarine
Equipment:
    mixing bowl, spoon or whisk, cheese grater, two 1-pound coffee cans and 1½-quart casserole

Mixing

Measure the **yeast, honey, salt, water,** and **milk powder** into your mixing bowl and stir well.
minute.

Mix in the **oil**.

Add **2 cups of flour** and stir well until you have a smooth, creamy mixture.

Beat the **egg** in well.

Cut the **cheese** into grater-size chunks and grate directly into the bowl. Don't mind if some bits of the cheese remain chunks instead of getting grated. Stir the cheese in well.

Add the **third cup of flour** and beat for 1 minute.

Add another **½ cup of flour** and beat for another

Add the **remaining flour** ½ cup at a time and work in well with your spoon or whisk. Because of the amount of flour, this recipe takes longer to work up than, say, Peanut Method Bread did, but it should still take less than an hour and a half altogether.

By the time you've worked in all the flour well, the batter is ready to turn into pans for baking. The batter will still look wettish—especially compared to the Peanut Method.

Filling the Cans

Grease well two 1-pound coffee cans and a 1½-quart casserole, filling each about one third full. If you don't have a casserole, make four 1-pound coffee can loaves, or simply use loaf pans.

Resting the Batter

Cover with clean towels and put into a very warm place to rise for 20 minutes. (Try the hot-water technique, p. 20. The two coffee cans will fit in a large spaghetti pot.)

There will only be a little rise after 20 minutes; not to worry.

Baking

Put into a cold oven and bake at a medium temperature (about 350°).

The 1-pound coffee cans take about 30 minutes, and are done when the top of the loaf begins to go brown. But test, don't guess (see pp. 21–23).

The casserole takes about 40 minutes to bake and forms a lovely golden-brown top when it's done. Again, turn the loaf out when you think it's done and test it.

Cool on a wire rack or bring it right to the table and tear it apart. You'll be glad you made more than one loaf.

Options

☞ Use more or less **cheese** to your taste; or try another kind of cheese.

☞ Try a Tan Cheese Bread, by using **2 cups of whole wheat flour** and 2½ cups of white for the total flour in the recipe.

☞ Substitute ½ cup of wheat germ (preferably raw) for ½ cup of the flour.

CHEESE METHOD BREAD—SUMMARY

A. 2 tbsp. active dry yeast
   3 tbsp. honey
   1 tbsp. sea salt
   2 cups hot water
   ⅔ cup skim milk powder

B. 2 tbsp. oil

C. 5 cups flour

D. 1 large egg

E. 6 oz. cheese

Measure A into a large mixing bowl and stir.

Add B.

Add 2 cups of C and mix well until smooth.

Add D and beat in well.

Grate in E and stir in well.

Add 1 cup of C and beat vigorously for 1 minute.

Beat in ½ cup of C for 1 minute.

Work in remains of C, ½ cup at a time, working in well.

Grease well two 1-pound coffee cans and a 1½-quart casserole, filling each about one third full.

Cover and rise in a warm place for 20 minutes. (Hot water recommended.)

Set in a cold oven and bake at 350° for 30 minutes for the coffee cans and 40 minutes for the casserole.

Knife-test for doneness.

Cool on a wire rack, or bring to the table hot.

METHOD SALLY LUNN

For flavor, texture, and seniority Sally Lunn is without doubt the queen of the Batter Breads.

Sally Lunn was an Englishwoman who is supposed to have sold these "cakes" in the resort town of Bath, sometime around the end of the eighteenth century.

And very like a European coffee cake it is: light and spongy in texture, yellow in color, with a flavor that is distinctively its own; it can be eaten plain, but is all the better for a sweet glaze; it is also one of the best toasters you will ever find. Or serve it with fruit preserves or honey and butter—even ice it as a cake.

Sally cuts well when hot—just use a serrated knife and saw gently; she even slices thin.

This is a perfect Method Bread for ring molds, or for long loaf pans. This recipe makes enough for two good-sized loaves or three rings.

One caution: Sally Lunn works up somewhat stickier than other New Method Breads. I handle this problem with a greased spoon and poke Sally into place and smooth the top easily.

Sally takes no longer than any other Method Bread—in fact, the last time I made it I made one ring and one large loaf: the ring was out in an *hour and fifteen minutes* from first measurement to turning out.

So by all means try this jewel of a Method Bread—and let your family eat cake.

METHOD SALLY LUNN

For Batter:
   2 tbsp. active dry yeast
   1 tsp. sea salt
   ⅓ cup honey
   1 cup hot water
   ⅓ cup skim milk powder
   ½ cup vegetable oil
   2 cups unbleached white flour (more to come)
   3 large eggs
   2 more cups unbleached white flour
For Greasing:
   butter or margarine
For Glaze:
   1 tbsp. honey
   juice of ½ orange
   peel of ½ orange, grated
Equipment:
   large mixing bowl, small bowl, 3 ring molds (or loaf
   pans), spoon

Mixing

Measure the **yeast, salt, honey, hot water,** and **milk powder** into a large bowl and mix well.

Stir in the **oil.**

Add **2 cups of flour,** mixing the whole into a paste.

Break in the **eggs** and mix until it's all smooth. (See Temperature of Ingredients, pp. 18–19.)

Add a **third cup of flour** and beat by hand for a few minutes, as vigorously as you can, or for 1 minute with an electric beater at medium speed.

Add the **remaining flour** ½ cup at a time, working it in very well. This working-in by spoon takes the place of beating, so don't skimp on it—there should be no excess flour visible on the bottom of the bowl or on the sides. When all the flour is worked in, the mixture should be elastic and ready; it will show that rubbery-sheeting look mentioned earlier. If you find the mixture too difficult to stir by spoon—*handle* it. All Method Breads are the better for extra handling.

Filling the Pans

Grease your pans well: three 8½" × 4½" × 2½" pans, or three 9-inch diameter by 2-inch depth ring molds, or two 12¾" × 4½" × 2½" pans—or some combination of pans and rings.

Turn the batter into the greased pans—which is easier said than done. This is a most cohesive batter and requires a great deal of urging to come out of its bowl. However, you can help the batter out with a greased spoon or spatula, or you can even use your greased hand.

With the same greased spoon, spatula, or hand, poke the batter into the corners of the pan. If you don't, you'll get air pockets—no great tragedy, but not desirable.

Try to smooth the batter out; tap down those peaks. If you leave them you get a rough top—also no tragedy.

With Sally Lunn it's especially important to remember to fill the pans *less than half full*. Sally rises. And the fuller the pan, the heavier the result.

Resting the Batter

Cover with a clean towel and put in a warm place for 20 minutes. The rising will be noticeable.

Baking

Start in a cold oven, set for medium-low, 350°.

Baking times will vary with the pans you use, from 30 minutes for ring molds, to 45 minutes for large pans.

Test with a toothpick for doneness (see p. 22).

Glazing

While the loaves are in the oven, gather together and combine into a small bowl **1 tablespoon of honey,** the **juice of ½ orange,** and the **peel of ½ orange,** grated.

When you have stirred the glaze ingredients together, pull the racks half out of the oven and spoon the glaze over the loaves. Do be gentle. Sally is a lady in a delicate condition at this stage, very susceptible to denting from rough handling. The glaze can go on any time during the baking—or afterwards if you forget. It doesn't really matter.

Return the rack to the oven to conclude the baking.

When done, the loaves will look a mixture of yellow, brown, and gold on top. So don't depend on color—test.

Cooling

Allow to cool in the pan for a few minutes, then turn out directly onto a serving plate, for serving hot.

Sally can bake while you are eating your dinner—and be served hot for dessert.

Options

☞ Use **1 cup of whole milk** instead of the hot water and skim milk powder, but if so, *warm the milk.*

☞ You might prefer **lemon** to orange for your glaze.

☞ For Method Holiday Bread (any holiday) add **4 ounces of chopped dried fruits** (pineapple, apricots, figs) to the batter after all the flour is in.

☞ **Raisins** and **chopped dates**—½ cup of fruit per loaf—make a Method Dressy Bread. If you use this combination, then glaze before baking: the glaze protects the raisins from burning.

☞ **Chopped nuts** can be added to Method Holiday Bread or Method Dressy Bread.

☞ Glazing is not mandatory; Sally is quite able to stand on her own, a delicate and sweet—but not too sweet—girl.

METHOD SALLY LUNN—SUMMARY

A. 1 tbsp. active dry yeast
   1 tsp. sea salt
   ⅓ cup honey
   1 cup hot water
   ⅓ cup skim milk
      powder

B. ½ cup vegetable oil

C. 4 cups flour

D. 3 large eggs
   1 tbsp. honey
   juice and peel of
      ½ orange

Measure A into a large mixing bowl and stir.

Add B.

Mix in 2 cups of C, and beat into a paste.

Mix in D until smooth.

Add 1 cup of C, and beat vigorously for a few minutes (1 minute by mixer).

Add the remaining C, ½ cup at a time, working in very well.

Grease three small pans well (rings are recommended).

Turn the batter into the greased pans, poke into corners, and smooth the surface with a greased hand or spoon. (Fill pans less than half full.)

Cover with a clean towel, and rise in a warm place for 20 minutes.

Set in a cold oven, and bake, medium-low (about 350°), for 30–45 minutes (depending on the pans).

Glaze, during baking, with a mixture of 1 tablespoon of honey and the juice and grated peel of ½ orange.

Test with a toothpick for doneness.

Some
Basic
Kneaded
Breads

Roll up your sleeves, take off your rings and watch, and get ready to knead; because here there be *bread*.

Don't mistake me: Method Breads are great when you're rushed. But when you have the time, there's nothing like kneaded breads.

In this chapter we'll work together through a few breads that will open the door to many. We'll do French Bread (my students' eyes always light up when I announce that we're about to do this one), Italian Bread (a more substantial cousin of French), and Refrigerator Rise Bread (excellent breads for working people on a tight schedule).

I know someone who calls kneaded breads "angry breads," because she can work out her temper on the dough—and the madder she feels, the better kneading she gives it. Well, I suppose she has a point. But you don't have to be pumping adrenalin to knead well. Nor do you have to be endowed with shot-putting muscles. Anyone can knead—the very young or the very old; the strong or the weak. For kneading doesn't depend on strength.

Kneading is a process in which you rub the particles of dough against one another to develop the elastic gluten (see p. 5).

This gluten can be formed very quickly by very vigorous handling, or it can be formed very slowly by gentle handling—a point worth emphasizing, because when I give a particular time for kneading (say, 10 minutes), I don't mean that you can tickle the dough for 10 minutes and expect to have the gluten developed and the bread ready for rising. You can get the gluten developed by tickling—but it will take you much longer. Contrariwise (as the caterpillar said to Alice), if you attack the dough as if it were your mother-in-law on a bad day, it will probably be fully kneaded in 5 minutes.

Techniques of kneading are almost as varied as people. Some like to poke or prod the dough with their fingers, some like to squeeze it between their fingers (a hangover, maybe, from mudpie days), some use mostly their palms, some prefer fists, some will combine these— all or any of the above will give you successful bread. In fact, any motion which rubs the particles of dough together will give you successful bread. What won't give you successful bread is tearing the dough apart. So don't pull. Use any motion in kneading that presses the dough onto itself, and avoid any motion that pulls it apart.

Comfort is awfully important in kneading. I had a student who came into class insisting that her arms got too tired to knead. Well, in my class everyone works. I told her to knead only until she got tired—and I had to pull her off the board. The magic? Her board at home was on a surface nearly a foot higher than mine. The board should be low enough so that you can pretty much straighten out your arms when you knead.

Most kneaders use a wooden board which they flour lightly through the kneading, but I use an old marble table top which I love—it requires much less flouring. Students with built-in counters tell me that formica tops are just as good as marble, and I've even heard of a large, heavy piece of glass being used for a kneading board.

I'm afraid that men have it all over women when it comes to kneading. Their hands are bigger, and their arms and shoulders generally more muscular, so their kneading can generally be done more quickly.

Don't be afraid to ask a friend or spouse for help in kneading. Some of the breads we do in this book (for example, Italian) require a lot of kneading, and are rather tiresome if you don't have someone to trade off with. But then, kneading doesn't have to be done all at one shot. You can knead for a bit, then cover the dough with a bowl, have a cup of herb tea, then knead some more. So long as the dough stays clean and doesn't dry out, you're fine.

I find a very good motion for kneading is to press the

dough against the kneading board with the heels of my hands, at the same time that I move it along the board a bit. Then, as I come to the end of my motion, to give a squeeze with my fingers—but that's only my preference: you have to find a motion that's comfortable for you. Experiment.

When I have completed a kneading motion, and the dough is rather thin on the board from being pressed and pushed, I fold it in half, and repeat my motion. By folding and repeating, I make certain that all parts of the dough are kneaded.

When dough sticks to your board (and it will), scrape it up and flour again on the clean board. Don't just flour over the stuck dough—you'll keep on sticking to the same place.

Kneading is something that's easier to do than to explain, so let's get into a bread and see how it works.

FRENCH BREAD

This is really a convertible bread (a hardtop convertible—it has a good crust). It has multi-ethnic origins. The way I'll treat it in this recipe it's French Bread, but I can buy the same bread, although much paler, in Spanish Harlem in New York, and it's Cuban Bread. On Nantucket it's almost white and is Portuguese Bread. Force in extra flour, and make a couple of minor changes (as we'll do in the next recipe), and you have Italian Bread. (When I first began to teach baking, I taught Cuban Bread as the first kneaded bread, but I got so many complaints about its natural paleness that I switched to French. You see, breads made with just water tend to be naturally pale—just as good, but pale. Breads made with shortening will become that golden color without any help.)

In its original form, this was truly a basic bread—flour, water, and yeast: you can't get any more basic than that. We've added salt to enhance the delicate flavor, and honey to give the yeast something to feed on quickly. Neither changes the basic nature of the bread.

The loaf you come up with here is something like the bread you might buy in a bakery—like a live bird is something like a stuffed bird. For in the bakery they can give you something that looks like real bread, and something that even feels like real bread (with a crisp crust), but for flavor bakery loaves don't compare to the French Bread you can make at home. You have to go to France to get French Bread this good (and I understand it's getting tougher to find good bread there, too).

The ingredients used in a commercial bakery just aren't as wholesome as those you use at home. They cut corners for profit; you don't have to. They use preservatives and chemical substitutes; you can use natural, wholesome ingredients. Furthermore, they make a loaf to suit the general public; you can make a loaf to suit your own taste.

Of course, the commercial baker has some advantages over the home baker, too. His oven gives uniform heat; I know mine and yours don't. He gets ample heat from the top as well as the bottom. We don't. And the baker of French Bread can use live steam in his oven—and this we can only approximate. But we'll do our best.

And our best will be pretty good.

We'll spray our loaves with water three times to give crust, and keep a pan of water in the bottom of the oven to raise the humidity during baking.

We'll use cornmeal on the baking sheets to give the loaves good, crunchy bottoms (that being the only part we can't spray).

We'll start with a cold oven to give the long strips of shaped dough plenty of chance to rise into high, light loaves.

All of which is considerably less trouble than it sounds. Especially for a bread which is not only tasty and a treat for the eyes, but the lowest calorie bread in this book.

FRENCH BREAD

For Dough:
    1½ tbsp. active dry yeast
    1 tbsp. honey
    1 tbsp. sea salt
    2 cups hot water
    6–7 cups unbleached white flour
For Greasing:
    melted butter or margarine
    sprinkling of cornmeal
Equipment:
    large mixing bowl, mixing spoon or whisk, kneading
    board, 2 baking sheets

Mixing

Into a large mixing bowl, measure the **yeast, honey,** and
salt. Mix. (As soon as yeast meets either honey or water,
you're making bread.)

Add the **hot water** (straight from the tap, if your tap
gives good hot water), and stir. The yeast hasn't dissolved
yet, but it is swelling and multiplying and making the
water cloudy.

Add about **2 cups of flour** and stir in with a whisk or
spoon.

Mix in **2 more cups of flour.** By now that spoon or
whisk is a hindrance, so clean it off into the bowl (see
pp. 12–13).

Add the **fifth cup of flour** and work it in with your
hand.

Dump the **sixth cup of flour** onto your kneading
board, spread it around, and scrape the dough out of the
bowl onto this flour. A rubber or plastic scraper is handy
for this transfer.

Kneading

Knead in this sixth cup of flour.

When the 6 cups of flour are worked in, you must
decide if there is enough flour in the dough—and so we
approach the moment of truth.

When there is enough flour, the dough will tend to
stop sticking to your hands and will allow itself to be
formed into a cohesive mass, something you can hold in
one hand, palm down, while it falls slowly to the board.

When there is enough flour, the dough will have a smooth feeling as you rub your hands over its surface.

If you feel the dough wants more flour (and if your hands aren't sticking I'd say it doesn't—for this light bread we want to use as little flour as we can get away with, not as much flour as we can force in), dump another ½ cup onto the board and work it in. This recipe should hold no less than 6 cups of flour—and no more than about 7 cups. If you go past 8 cups you're on your way to Italian Bread (delicious, too, but something else, as you'll see when we get to it).

When the dough has enough flour, *continue to knead for another 10 minutes.* The dough should work easily. A light dusting of flour on the board now and then is a help—but that means a light dusting of flour, not a thick layer. Just enough to keep your dough from adhering to the board.

As you knead, you'll feel the resistance of the dough change from soft as pudding to something that actually seems to be pushing back against your hands. From being utterly pliant, it becomes something that wants to keep its own shape.

When you feel resistance grow, you're getting there.

After 10 minutes, the dough should have quite a smooth feel to it, and should show, when you look at a surface, the characteristic "wrinkles" that indicate when a dough has been kneaded enough. These "wrinkles" make the surface of the dough look somewhat like a textured paint job—not rough or coarse, just faintly textured.

If you're not sure after 10 minutes, knead for a few minutes more and look again. You can't hurt a bread by kneading too much, but if you don't knead enough, the dough won't hold its shape well in the loaf—it will sag, which seems a rather drastic way to find out that you haven't kneaded enough.

First Rise

After you've admired your kneaded ball of dough for a little while, pour a few drops of oil (or melted butter or margarine) into the same mixing bowl (you needn't wash it); put the ball of dough in; turn the dough over to oil the other sides; cover the bowl with a clean towel; and place

it in a draft-free, warm place to rise for about an hour
(see Rising Dough, pp. 19–21).

The rising time will depend on several variables (the
general temperature of your kitchen, the warmth right
under your bowl, the heaviness of your dough—to name
a few), so rather than depending on a specific timing, use
these guides: (1) look at the ball of dough—it will look
much risen, taking up more than twice as much room in
the bowl; and (2) when it looks that much bigger, use the
finger test.

Finger Test

Gently insert into the dough (not in the center but near
the side of the bowl where there is less surface tension
and things are less dry) one or two fingers, *halfway to the
first knuckle*—about half an inch. Wiggle them gently—
to free them from the sticky dough—and draw them out
again. Now watch. If the indentation you've made remains
more or less intact, the dough has risen enough to "punch
down." If the hole gradually fills itself, re-cover the bowl
and let the dough rise for a while longer (say, 15 minutes).

If you attempt to bake bread that hasn't risen sufficiently, you'll get hard, heavy stuff—great for doorstops
and for heaving through windows during riots, but no
treat for you or your family. (There are places you can
skimp in baking—I know I cut a lot of time corners in my
classes because I've just got to get all the breads on the
schedule finished before it gets late. But one place I have
learned never to skimp is in the time for the first rise.)

Make certain, when you're finger testing, that you
don't poke too strongly or too deeply. If you do, it will be
like puncturing a balloon and you'll have to knead it all
down and begin to rise your dough all over again.

OK, that's no tragedy. It can happen that a cat sits
on the towel and punches it down for you prematurely.
As long as your dough is still clean, you have lost nothing
but time. Work it back to its original size and let it rise
until it passes the finger test.

Remember, the speed of this first rise depends on the
bowl being kept warm and out of drafts (the towel helps
keep the drafts out and the heat in): in a cool place it can

take all day to rise. So, if you wish, you can deliberately leave your dough in a nonwarm place and go out to the movies, expecting it to be sufficiently risen by the time you get back. Bread making doesn't chain you to the oven.

It happens sometimes, while you are at the movies, that your dough will rise as much as it wants, and then fall of its own accord. (You can tell because the dough adheres to the sides of the bowl, but sags in the middle.) Fine. Bakeries sometimes use this voluntary collapse to tell when their dough is ready to punch down. If that happens to you, you can skip the finger test because the dough has done it for itself.

Punching Down

When the dough has risen enough, make a fist and punch it down. When I say "punch it down," that's what you really do; make a fist and punch down through the risen dough. The dough will make a soft hissing noise as the gas is forced out, and that's what you're trying to do—get out most of the gas that's just been released into the bread from the yeast action.

Knead out the rest of the gas bubbles—either in the bowl or on your kneading board. (The dough shouldn't be sticky, but a light flouring of the board will help if it is.) This should take no more than a minute or so. Now you're not kneading to develop the gluten, but, rather, squeezing to get rid of the larger bubbles—all this to give you an even texture.

Shaping the Loaves

This recipe will make four fair-sized loaves. Cut the dough into four pieces. Don't be misled by the apparent smallness of the pieces of dough—they will really rise.

With your hands starting in the center, roll the pieces in long, thin "baguettes" about 1½ inches thick, the traditional shape for French Bread.

If you prefer, make some other shape that appeals to you: round for Portuguese Bread, eight small pieces for individual loaves, or even smaller for *Petits Pains* (see Options, pp. 58–59).

Grease two baking sheets and then sprinkle them

lightly with **yellow cornmeal,** shaking the pan from side to side make an even layer.

Place the shaped loaves onto these sheets, leaving plenty of room for them to rise and spread. You don't want the loaves to touch in the baking.

Again cover with clean, dry towels, and again put them into a warm, draft-free place to rise.

Second Rise

This bread, as any classic kneaded bread, takes a second rise after being shaped into loaves. Given the same warmth, this second rise takes about half as long as the first.

I don't use a test to tell me whether or not the loaves are risen enough; when they are ready *they will look almost twice as large*—taking up about twice as much room on the sheets. (Some experts recommend using a finger test on the loaves, but that finger mark stays in the finished loaf, and I don't like to mar my loaves. Besides, *this* rise can be skimped a little—if really necessary.)

The loaves get quite large in the rising—even larger in the baking—and if they touch each other (I warned you about leaving room) better not try to separate them; you're more likely to punch them down—which means more rising time. If, by mischance, they do get punched down, just reshape them into loaves and start again from there.

These re-starts don't mean that you double your rising time. The yeast is still growing, which means that *each subsequent rising takes less time.* (Gourmets like their bread to have three or even four risings in the bowl—and each is faster than the previous rise.)

When the loaves are risen you'll want to slash them and slather on cold water. You slash with a very sharp or serrated knife, making your cuts diagonally (to make the loaf rise *up* in the baking, rather than *out*—Viennese Bread is a long, oval loaf slashed down the center to grow very wide; don't do that here), three or four cuts per loaf. Make your slashes *very gently*, cutting only about $\frac{1}{8}$-$\frac{1}{4}$ inch into the loaf—with a serrated knife, just a bit more than the depth of the serrations. If you cut deeply, you'll burst that balloon again. (If you're making round loaves, slash them in the shape of a cross, or like tic-tac-toe, or like the spokes of a wheel.)

Once the cuts are made, slather the surface with cold

water, sprayed from your plant sprayer or laundry sprayer or applied gently with your fingers or a clean brush. This water helps in crust and color formation.

Baking

Boil up a cup or so of water and put it in an open container in the bottom of the oven (I use an old cake pan). The evaporation of this water (simulating steam in a brick oven) also helps in crust formation.

Put the loaves into a *cold* oven (this gives the yeast an extra chance to do its thing), nearer to the top than the bottom, light, and set your flame for about 400°—medium-high if you don't have a thermometer or thermostat.

Bake for about 30–40 minutes.

During the baking (after 10 minutes and again after 15 minutes) slide the loaves forward from the oven for two more sprayings or brushings of cold water. (This gives you a chance to admire how nice and big they are now.)

Bottom color is a better guide to doneness for this loaf than top color. You can get a brown top by reflectance. If you are using aluminum baking trays, the shiny bottom of the upper one reflects heat down onto the top of the lower tray, and the lower loaf can get a browner crust from this reflection.

When the bottom of a loaf shows darkish golden brown, take a loaf out of the oven and turn it upside down on a clean towel and knife-test it for doneness (see pp. 21–23).

If the loaves test done but are too pale for you, put them under the broiler flame or coil (at high) for 30 seconds—a minute will probably be too long, so watch that second hand—and the loaves will have brown tops, too.

Stand the loaves on a wire rack to cool.

By all means eat the bread hot, tearing off chunks in the French manner. This bread is never again so good as it is when hot from the oven.

Options

☞ The first thing to learn about this or any bread is that the taste to please is yours and that of your family. And one of the most variable tastes is that for salt. By all

means, if you like a saltier loaf, add more salt to the recipe
or use salty water for your spraying.

☞ This is a water bread, but the "water" you use
can vary enormously; it can be vegetable water as well as
tap water. If you boil vegetables the water winds up with
most of the vitamins anyhow, so it makes good sense to
use it for cooking. And don't think it has to be bland or
thin "water" either. I've used a rich chicken soup for
"water" and been very happy with the result.

Of course, if you're using a salty "water," adjust the
amount of salt you use in the recipe.

☞ Another method for achieving the crust on
French Bread uses the same recipe, but when the loaf has
been in for about 20–25 minutes (about 15 minutes before
the loaf is done), glaze the tops with an egg white, then
sprinkle sesame seeds over the glazed surfaces.

☞ Whole wheat flour can be substituted for about
two thirds of the white flour—though it works up best
half and half. Put in the white first, then add the whole
wheat flour a cup at a time. You'll find that you use less
flour in total for the same amount of liquid—whole wheat
flour absorbs more liquid than white. (See Chapter 4.)

☞ By all means substitute 1 cup of raw wheat
germ for the white flour: you'll be putting back much of
what the miller took out. If you aren't sure how you'll like
this change, substitute only half a cup of wheat germ the
first time. But do *substitute* or you will get heavy bread.
(Put the wheat germ in as the fourth or fifth cup.)

☞ Petits Pains (literally, little breads) are individual small loaves, made up exactly like the larger
breads. (It's really a great moment when you can set one
at each guest's place for a dinner party.) When the dough
has completed its first rise, divide it into twelve pieces
(rather than four), and shape each piece into an oval loaf
about 6 inches long. Space them out on the baking sheets
(remember, they will spread), rise them, spray, and bake,
just like the full-sized loaves. They will bake up sooner—
but only a *little* sooner.

Another method for getting color on the *Petits Pains*
is to use an egg-white and water glaze (1 egg white mixed
with 1 teaspoon of water). As soon as the *Petits Pains* are
shaped into loaves, brush them with the egg glaze and
sprinkle with sesame seeds.

The finished little breads will thump hollow, but do test at least one or two from each tray to make certain.

☞ This bread gets stale rather quickly (3–4 days); that's a characteristic of water breads. So you might want to bake only a part of the dough, and save the rest for later in the week. Nothing is simpler. Put the dough you didn't bake into the fridge in a covered bowl. The dough will rise, even in the cold, but that's all to the good: the more risings the better the texture. When you want the dough, take it from the fridge, punch it down, knead out the larger air bubbles, and allow it to come to room temperature before shaping into a loaf (or, you can shape immediately and allow extra time for the cold loaf to rise).

☞ If you add **2 tablespoons of vegetable oil** to the recipe, your bread won't stale quite as fast.

FRENCH BREAD—SUMMARY

A. 1½ tbsp. active dry yeast   B. 6–7 cups flour
   1 tbsp. honey
   1 tbsp. sea salt
   2 cups hot water

Into a large bowl measure and mix together A.

Mix in the first 5 cups of B.

Spread sixth cup over board, dump batter onto board, and knead with as much additional flour as required to stop sticking.

Knead another 10 minutes after all the flour is in.

Return to oiled bowl, cover, and set to rise in a warm place for an hour.

Finger-test.

When sufficiently risen, punch down, knead out the larger air bubbles.

Cut the dough into four pieces, shape into loaves, and place on greased, cornmealed baking sheets.

Cover loaves with a clean towel and put in a warm place to rise until doubled in size. (Do not test.)

Slash the loaves and water them.

Boil water and put it in the bottom of the stove. (Do not preheat oven.)

Put to bake for about 40 minutes at about 400°—medium-high.

Water again after 10 and after 15 minutes of baking.

Test by knife.

Cool on a wire rack. Eat hot—tearing rather than cutting.

ITALIAN BREAD

We use the words "French Bread" and "Italian Bread" as if these were the sole breads ever eaten in France and Italy. Actually, there's a wide spectrum of French and Italian Breads (see Brioches, pp. 154–162, for example). In a way, these two breads are poverty breads—that is, they are made of the cheapest ingredients (no expensive grains, no expensive additions).

Although they are presented here separately, the breads of these two nationalities have much in common, as you'll see in this recipe. The true national difference is the amount of flour—that is, the French generally work with soft and the Italians with stiff dough.

Italian Bread is work. Don't fool yourself that it's not. This is a bread that I have my husband knead for me. But if you want a substantial, dense, and delicious peasant bread, here it is.

If you are buying olive oil for this bread, or for any other part of your Italian dinner, watch out—you have to read the label. If the label says "virgin" you're all right, because many of the original vitamins will be intact. If the label says "pure" it is a more processed oil and is missing important nutrients. However, olive oil is used largely for flavor. For nutrition pick an oil higher in linoleic acid—say corn or soy oil.

This is the most difficult kneading of any of the breads in this book: it is the driest dough. And yet it should rise without difficulty.

ITALIAN BREAD

For the Dough:
2 tbsp. active dry yeast
1 tbsp. honey
2 cups hot water
1½ tbsp. sea salt
¼ cup vegetable (or olive) oil
8–9 cups unbleached white flour
For Greasing:
melted butter or margarine
cornmeal for sprinkling
Equipment:
large mixing bowl, mixing spoon, 2 baking sheets, would you believe an electric fan?, and an optional rolling pin

Mixing

Into a large mixing bowl measure **2 tablespoons of yeast** and **1 tablespoon of honey.**

Add **2 cups of hot tap water** and **1½ tablespoons of salt,** and stir until the salt is dissolved. (The yeast will probably look clumpy: don't fret, we've a long way to go.)

Add **¼ cup of vegetable (or olive) oil** and stir in.

Mix in the **first 4 cups of flour,** 2 cups at a time, stirring in with your spoon or a wire whisk.

Mix in the **next 2 cups of flour,** right in the bowl, though you'll probably want to switch to working with your hand rather than a spoon. It's at this point that we start kneading.

Dump **a seventh cup of flour** onto the board, and scrape the batter out of the bowl, onto the flour. Knead in well.

Measure **an eighth cup** and dump it on the board. Knead in well. No, I'm not kidding. The dough will take that eighth cup *and more.*

If you can manage it, add another **½ cup of flour** and knead in. (If you can't manage it, the bread will still be Italian.) If it's a damp day, add flour all the way to 9 cups —be a hero.

Once this last flour is well kneaded in, you already have cohesion, that is, you can hold up the dough ball in one hand, palm down, and it won't fall; now knead for another 5 or 10 minutes.

This is a very resistant dough—one you can almost stand on. And that resistance gives the clue to when it's ready. Shape the dough into a rough ball and press it against the board. If, despite your pressure, the ball wants to stay a few inches thick, then it's ready to put to rise. At this point, the dough should stick to nothing.

First Rise

Pour a few drops of oil (or melted butter or margarine) into the same bowl, drop in the ball of dough, turn it over a few times to make sure it's oiled all over, cover with a clean, wet towel, and put into a very warm, draft-free place to rise for *about* an hour (see pp. 19–21).

When the ball of dough looks quite risen, give it the finger test as described in French Bread, p. 54.

Punching Down

If the dough is ready, punch it down and knead gently for a moment to get rid of the larger air bubbles. The dough should feel easier to handle.

Shaping the Loaves

Learn the following procedure for getting a good web with this heavy bread, and you can use it to improve any kneaded bread you care to make.

Divide the dough into three pieces and shape each piece into a ball.

Lay a piece on your kneading board and, poking it

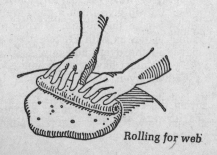

Rolling for web

with your fingers stiff, begin to flatten it into a rectangle. This whole process can be done with your bare hands, poking and pressing the dough thinner and thinner until it's about 10 by 12 inches and ½ inch thick; or, once you get the dough reasonably flat, you can switch to a rolling pin. Turning the dough over every so often makes it easier to handle, and less likely to stick.

Now, starting from the longer side of the rectangle, roll as tightly as you can manage, rolling the dough into a long, thick cigar. (The loaf will probably be about 2 inches thick and long enough to stretch right across your baking sheet.)

When you've got the cigar, pinch the ends closed and tuck them under (to look neat) and pinch the seam closed (otherwise the bread will unroll in the baking). Repeat to make the other two loaves.

Grease a pair of large baking sheets and sprinkle them with **yellow cornmeal,** shaking the sheets from side to side to get an even layer.

Lay the loaves on the sheets seam side down, as far apart as possible, to leave room for spreading and rising.

With a sharp knife, slash to a depth of almost ½ inch, three or four long diagonal slashes.

Using your fingers or a pastry brush or a sprayer, wet the surface of the loaves.

Cover with clean, dry towels and put to rise in a very warm place for one half to three quarters of an hour.

Baking

When risen (the slashes will gape wide), put a cup or so of water on to boil.

Once again spray or brush the loaves with cold water. Don't drown them, but do give them a good wetting.

Put a shallow pan in the bottom of your oven and pour in the boiling water, as with French Bread.

Put the loaves in the oven, and *now* light. For this heavy bread the yeast must have every chance to work.

Bake in a medium oven, around 350°–375° for 30–40 minutes.

Twice during the baking (at 10 and at 15 minutes) pull the loaves forward and again spray or brush them with water.

Crackling

When the loaves test done (see pp. 21–23), remove them from the oven and stand them on a wire rack. Now, believe it or not, if you want that crackled crust that is so typical of Italian Bread, cool the loaves in the breeze from an electric fan!

Eat the bread as hot as you can get it after the fanning. And don't worry about that old wives' tale about the unhealthiness of eating hot bread. It's true that when a loaf is very hot, and you cut it open with a dullish knife, or you press a bit of dough between your fingers, it seems raw. But it isn't; raw dough looks drippy. There is still a good deal of moisture in a fresh-baked hot loaf, but it can't do you any harm at all.

So do eat your bread hot, when it's at its tastiest.

Options

☞   Substitute **1 cup of raw wheat germ** for a cup of white flour. (Make the substitution for any of the first 6 cups.)

☞   Substitute **whole wheat flour** for any amount of white, up to about 50 percent. (As the whole wheat flour is more absorbent, expect to use a total of about 7½–8½ cups of flour.)

☞   For a small adventure you might try a bread I call "Soychick" Bread. In this Italian Bread recipe, substitute for the water either **chicken soup** or the water left after cooking up a pot of chick peas (**chick-pea water** is quite flavorful). Then, substitute a cup of **soy flour** for a cup of white flour—late in the kneading (say, about cup no. 7). This is very rich for a water bread, high in protein from the soy, a mellow color, and one of the best toasters you'll ever find.

☞   Parma Bread. Add to the bowl **6 tablespoons of grated Parmesan cheese.**

If you want cheese in only one or two loaves, knead in 2 tablespoons of cheese per loaf after dividing into loaves. Make sure you knead the cheese in well.

After the final spraying, that is, after 15 minutes of baking, sprinkle the loaves with additional Parmesan.

☞   **Egg glaze** (see French Bread, p. 58). With this bread, the seeds for the glaze can be either sesame or poppy. Whenever I glaze, I seed: it's a waste to have that sticky egg surface and not put seeds on it. I prefer poppy seeds for Italian Rolls (follow the directions for *Petits Pains*, pp. 58–59).

☞ *Pane di San Giuseppe* (Saint Joseph's Bread) is made by adding **6 tablespoons of anise seed** after the hot water (and you've got to like anise for this one), and then shaping the loaf to resemble a patriarch's beard. (Though no one will stop you from making more conventional loaves and using a simple egg glaze.) On March 19, bring your beard-shaped loaf over to the *Festa di San Giuseppe* for blessing (most of us can use all the help we can get).

☞ Bread sticks are popular with young and old, and easy to have on hand because they keep better than loaves. Tear off walnut-sized balls of risen and punched-down dough. Roll these balls into strips a little thinner than your little finger. Pinch the ends smooth and lay on a greased baking sheet to rise (about half the time of the previous rise). Brush with milk, for color; and sprinkle on coarse salt—kosher salt or coarse sea salt. Bake at about 350° for 12–15 minutes or until a satisfactory golden-brown color. Eat one or two to make sure they are done.

☞ The most common Garlic Bread is made with a finished loaf of bread. Simply slice the loaf through lengthwise (that is, parallel to the cutting board) and smear the halves with **garlic butter** (made by mashing 1 or 2 cloves of garlic in ¼ cup of butter or margarine). Roll in aluminum foil and bake until heated through, about 10 minutes.

To make a Garlic Bread *baked with garlic*, add 2 tablespoons (or more) of **dried garlic flakes** after the hot water, and make up as you would the normal recipe.

ITALIAN BREAD—SUMMARY

A. 2 tbsp. active dry yeast   B. 8–9 cups flour
    1 tbsp. honey
    2 cups hot water
    1½ tbsp. sea salt
    ¼ cup oil

Into a large bowl measure and mix A.
Mix first 6 cups of B into a bowl, 2 cups at a time.

Spread another cup on kneading board and scrape out dough onto board.

Knead in the eighth cup.

Knead in as much of the last cup as you can, until the dough is very stiff and very resistant to kneading, then knead for another 5 or 10 minutes.

Cover with a clean wet towel and put to rise for about an hour.

When risen (as shown by a finger test), punch down, and shape into three long loaves.

Grease two baking sheets and sprinkle with cornmeal.

Lay the loaves on the sheets and slash three or four times per loaf, diagonally, almost ½ inch deep.

Spray with water and put to rise, covered, in a very warm place.

Boil up some water, and put in a shallow container on the bottom of the oven.

When the loaves are risen, spray again. Bake at about 350°–375° for 30–40 minutes.

Spray a third and fourth time after baking for 10 minutes and 15 minutes.

Test. Cool on a wire rack in a draft (for the Italian crackle). Eat hot.

REFRIGERATOR RISE BREADS

For some of my students, this is the basic bread: it's the only one their kids will eat, because it's the one that looks most like what they've been conditioned to by television.

Refrigerator Rise Bread is a favorite bread with people on a tight schedule. It can be made up (just kneaded and shaped) in the evening, kept in the refrigerator overnight (where it rises—hence, the name Refrigerator Rise), and in the morning popped into the oven to have hot and fresh with breakfast.

This isn't an original concept with me: Robin Hood flour has an entire leaflet devoted to it and Fleischmann's yeast has a recipe for a Cool Rise Bread in its recipe booklet. You can also make up your own Refrigerator Rise recipes, or adapt this or others to your likes.

We'll do two of these breads in this section: Wheat Germ Refrigerator Rise, and Oatmeal Refrigerator Bread, which, with the options, covers quite a bit of ground. In addition, see Refrigerator Rye in Chapter 7.

These are moist doughs, made with oil. In fact, whatever other options, changes, and variations you try, *don't leave out the oil*, because it's the oil that makes this kind of bread possible. It's the oil that allows the little bit of dough you put into the fridge in a baking pan to expand to almost three times its size by the time you take it out of the oven, and it's the oil that enables it to rise so well in the fridge.

Let me fill you in on the mechanics of this kind of bread.

First, you mix and knead it, like any kneaded bread, keeping a soft, moist dough, but one that doesn't stick.

Second, you divide it into loaf pans and put the loaves into the fridge to rise (a minimum of 5 hours, a maximum of 24).

Third, you take the loaves out and bake them.

As you can see, it's a simple procedure, with no testing or guessing about whether or not the bread is sufficiently risen—you can see it's risen, and you can know that if it's been rising for 5 to 24 hours, it's risen enough.

These breads have coarser webs than kneaded breads with two rises. French Bread has small, fairly even bubbles—we say that it has an even or smooth web. The pattern of the bubbles in Refrigerator Rise is uneven; largish bubbles tending toward the top of the bread and the smaller ones toward the bottom—making a coarse web. Occasionally these bubbles form right under the skin of the rising dough. When such blisters do form, prick them with a sharp fork, or pinch them between your fingers before baking the bread.

A shortcoming of Refrigerator Rise is that if you leave it too long in the fridge it may collapse; then it must be kneaded down and re-risen—which can take a while.

In my refrigerator I find the loaves subject to all kinds of minor accidents—a zucchini falls from an upper shelf, or my husband drops a loaf while taking something out of the refrigerator. But then, perhaps you're more careful than we are. Any zucchini marks, or what have you, stay in the bread.

When you put the loaves in the fridge, cover them

with oiled plastic wrap or waxed paper. If you don't grease the papers they will stick to the tops of the loaves and partly punch them down. Which means either you re-shape and re-rise or you settle for flat-topped bread. So, grease.

WHEAT GERM REFRIGERATOR RISE

> For the Dough:
>   2 tbsp. active dry yeast
>   2 tbsp. honey
>   1 tbsp. sea salt
>   2 cups hot water
>   ⅔ cup instant skim milk powder
>   ½ cup vegetable oil
>   4 cups unbleached white flour
>   1 cup raw wheat germ
>   1–2 more cups unbleached white flour
> For Greasing:
>   melted margarine or butter
> Equipment:
>   large mixing bowl, mixing spoon or whisk, kneading board, 3 baking pans (8½" × 4½" × 2½"), plastic wrap or wax paper

Mixing

Into a large bowl mix together **2 tablespoons of yeast, 2 tablespoons of honey, 1 tablespoon of salt,** and **2 cups of hot tap water.** Stir to dissolve the salt.

Add ⅔ **cup of instant skim milk powder** (or ⅓ cup of the non-instant) and stir.

Mix in ½ **cup of vegetable oil.** (Here I would not recommend olive oil—unless you really enjoy the flavor.)

Stir in the **first 4 cups of flour,** 2 cups at a time.

When that's all wetted, stir in **1 cup of raw wheat germ.**

Kneading

Spread **1 cup of flour** over your kneading board, scrape the batter from the bowl onto the board, and work the flour in.

When this is all worked in, you will probably want to knead in, say, ½ **cup more,** plus sprinklings on the board to keep it from sticking. This should end up as a soft (not sticky), moist dough, so don't force flour to the point where it is dry: stop as soon as the dough can be handled without sticking.

When you have enough flour in the dough, knead for an easy 10 minutes.

Let the dough rest on the board while you grease three 8½" × 4½" × 2½" baking pans with melted butter or margarine. *Don't substitute oil for greasing with this bread: the oil gets absorbed during the long rise, and the bread will stick.*

Cut the dough into three pieces and shape three loaves to fit the pans. (You can use the same flattening and rolling technique that we discussed in Italian Bread on pp. 56–57.)

If you want good, smooth end slices, chop down with the edge of your hand as near as possible to the end of the loaf. This karate chop will leave a small ridge of dough. Fold this ridge under, and repeat for the other side.

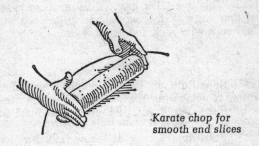

Karate chop for smooth end slices

Oil (or grease with melted butter or margarine) three pieces of plastic wrap to fit over the pans, and cover loosely.

Rising

We don't put these loaves into the usual "warm, draft-free place" to rise; we put them into a *cold*, draft-free place—your refrigerator.

Be sure that there's some room above the pans, for the dough will rise above the top, and then some.

Also, put the pans in a position where they won't

have to be moved around. A fingerprint made in the dough stays there (though even dented loaves come out looking beautiful).

Allow to rise for a minimum of 5 hours and a maximum of 24 hours. Like almost everything else in baking, this is an approximation: I have baked Refrigerator Rise after only 2 hours in the fridge; and I have occasionally seen it hold its shape for as much as 36 hours in the fridge—but don't count on it.

Baking

Remove from the refrigerator, take off the plastic gently, light your oven, and put the loaves in. It is not necessary to bring them to room temperature, but you may.

Bake at 325°–350° for about 50 minutes. But since this bread has a tendency to bake in more or less time than one expects, keep your nose peeled (see pp. 22–23).

When the crust is dark brown, test for doneness (see pp. 21–23). This is a taller bread than most, so be certain you get that knife all the way *almost* to the top.

Cool on a wire rack and serve warm.

Options

☞ Substitute up to half **whole wheat flour** for the white, remembering that since the whole wheat is more absorbent, you'll wind up using less flour for the same amount of liquid.

☞ Substitute **2 cups of whole milk** for the milk powder and hot water if you are baking for kids. Or use super-milk, that is, 2 cups of whole milk *plus* milk powder. As I've said before, you have to have *hot* liquid for good yeast action, so heat the milk.

☞ A **half cup of raisins** or more for the recipe, kneaded in when shaping the loaves, makes a very nice addition.

☞ The addition of ¼ cup of **sesame seeds** or **sunflower seeds** is a good variation.

WHEAT GERM REFRIGERATOR RISE—SUMMARY

A. 2 tbsp. active dry yeast
   2 tbsp. honey
   1 tbsp. sea salt
   2 cups hot water

B. ⅔ cup skim milk powder

C. ½ cup vegetable oil

D. 5–6 cups flour

E. 1 cup raw wheat germ

Combine A into a large mixing bowl and stir.
Mix in B, then C.
Stir in 4 cups of D (2 cups at a time).
Work in E.
Spread fifth cup of D on kneading board; scrape out batter onto board, and knead in.
Knead in as much of a sixth cup as wanted.
Knead for 10 minutes more.
Divide and shape into three loaves.
Grease three 8½″ × 4½″ × 2½″ baking pans.
Put the loaves into the pans, cover each with a piece of greased plastic wrap, and put into the refrigerator to rise for 5–24 hours.
At baking time, remove plastic, bake at 325°–350° for about 50 minutes.
Test, cool on a wire rack, and eat warm.

OATMEAL REFRIGERATOR BREAD

With this bread we use yogurt as a baking ingredient for the first time.

I use homemade yogurt. It's easy to make and inexpensive.

Begin with a container of plain yogurt whose flavor you like (one without preservatives); mix a cup of it with a cup of reconstituted powdered milk, and put it in a warm place to "work." The yogurt will have solidified overnight and you'll have 2 cups of yogurt, which either has to be refrigerated or put to "work" again. Now, anytime you want to increase your yogurt, add milk again and put the mixture over gentle heat, and there it is—yogurt as good as the commercial kind and for pennies a cup. Make your own buttermilk the same way.

Go on—drive the dairy trust wild.

The recipe calls for 5 to 5½ cups of flour, but the amount of flour will depend on the brand of oatmeal you use (different brands have different absorptions).

Be sure not to use instant—the recipe has been worked out with real oatmeal. In fact, avoid all instant foods. That instant stuff has been precooked, or pre-softened, using heat that destroys whatever vitamins are left after the first processing.

OATMEAL REFRIGERATOR BREAD

For the Dough:
 1½ cups oatmeal (not instant)
 1½ cups boiling water
 ⅓ cup vegetable oil
 ⅓ cup honey
 2 tbsp. active dry yeast
 1 tbsp. sea salt
 1 cup yogurt (or buttermilk)
 5–5½ cups unbleached white flour
 ¼ cup raw wheat germ
For Greasing:
 melted butter or margarine
Equipment:
 large mixing bowl, mixing spoon or whisk, kneading board, 3 baking pans 8½″ × 4½″ × 2½″, plastic wrap

Mixing

Over **1½ cups of oatmeal**, pour **1½ cups of boiling water** and stir to wet down all the oatmeal.

Into the same cup measure **⅓ cup of vegetable oil** and **⅓ cup of honey.** Pour over the oatmeal and stir in, scraping the cup to get out all the liquid.

Stir in **2 tablespoons of yeast,** then **1 tablespoon of salt** and **1 cup of yogurt** or buttermilk.

When the first seven ingredients are well mixed, add the **first 4 cups of flour,** 2 cups at a time, working it in well.

Mix in **¼ cup of raw wheat germ.**

Pour **1 cup of flour** (#5) onto the kneading board, scrape the batter onto the board, and work the flour in. This is a stickier batter than the Wheat Germ Refrigerator Rise, but resist the temptation to use large amounts of additional flour. Scrape your hands clean of batter, if necessary, and knead.

When the dough stops sticking, it has enough flour. Now knead for another 10 minutes.

Grease three 8½″ × 4½″ × 2½″ baking pans.

Divide the dough into thirds and shape three loaves.

Put the loaves into the pans, cover each loosely with a piece of greased wax paper or plastic, and put into the fridge.

Rising

Allow the loaves to rise in the fridge for 5–24 hours, without handling or punching them down.

Baking

When risen, take from the fridge, remove the plastic wrap, and bake at 350°–400° for around 40 minutes.

Test for doneness (see pp. 21–23).

Cool on a wire rack. Eat some warm; the rest will be good for days.

Options

☞ Like its near relative, Wheat Germ Refrigerator Rise, this bread can take ½ cup of raisins or ¼ cup of sesame seeds or sunflower seeds, kneaded into the loaves just before shaping.

OATMEAL REFRIGERATOR BREAD—SUMMARY

A. 1½ cups oatmeal
   1½ cups boiling water

B. ⅓ cup vegetable oil
   ⅓ cup honey

C. 2 tbsp. active dry yeast
   1 tbsp. sea salt
   1 cup yogurt
      (or buttermilk)

D. 5–5½ cups flour

E. ¼ cup raw wheat germ

Into a large mixing bowl combine A and stir well.
Add B and mix in.
Add C and stir.

Measure in first 4 cups of D, 2 cups at a time.

Work in E.

Spread another cup of D over the board and scrape batter onto the board. Knead in, adding as much more as required to keep dough from sticking.

Knead 10 minutes more.

Grease three baking pans, $8\frac{1}{2}'' \times 4\frac{1}{2}'' \times 2\frac{1}{2}''$.

Shape the dough into three loaves and put into the pans.

Cover with greased plastic wrap and set in the refrigerator to rise for 5–24 hours.

When you want to bake, remove plastic, and bake at 350°–400° for about 40 minutes.

Test for doneness.

Cool on a wire rack. Eat warm.

☞ 4 ☜

Whole
Wheat
Bread

Like a canoeist who has passed over some rocky shoals without getting a whole punched in his bottom, I breathe a deep sigh and pass from white breads that have to be *made* healthy, to Whole Wheat Breads. This is where *we* live.

These breads need no help—so long as you buy whole wheat flour which is untreated (not brominated, for example) and which is stone ground. These two conditions met, your whole wheat flour should have a broad range of vitamins and minerals and proteins, from both the germ and the bran.

We consider these our everyday breads, and so, I hope, will you. They are certainly tasty enough to be a daily favorite, and very healthful.

There are a few differences in handling whole wheat dough that are worth mentioning. For one thing, the raw whole wheat dough tends to form a crust easily, and so must be kept covered with a *wet*, clean towel while rising in the bowl. (Soak a towel with hot tap water and wring it out.) This will keep a damp atmosphere around the dough and prevent the surface from drying out. You could use a damp towel over all doughs, but for whole wheat it's a must.

Whole wheat flour is more absorbent than white flour (even than wheat germ flour), and so you'll use less flour for the same amount of liquid—keep that fact in mind when you are adapting or inventing your own recipes.

In kneading Whole Wheat Bread there is a different feel to the dough. White flour dough is more or less equally moist on the surface and inside the dough ball. But with whole wheat, the outside can feel dry, sticking

neither to the board nor to your hands, yet if you poke
your fingers inside it's sticky enough that you begin to
wonder if you don't need at least another cup of flour to
dry it out. Well, *don't* dry it out! It's supposed to feel
moist inside. If you were to force in enough flour to make
it feel like white flour dough, you'd wind up with a hor-
ribly heavy bread.

Whole Wheat Breads don't rise as high as white
breads, so don't expect them to. Nor can they give you as
fine and delicate a texture. But these are kneaded breads,
and, as kneaded breads, will give you good texture (just
not quite as fluffy as white). Because of this tendency toward heaviness, we like to give our Whole Wheat Breads
a bit of extra kneading. By doing this, and by working on
the wet side, you can wind up with a surprisingly light,
all-purpose bread.

If you've tried one or two other kneaded breads these
Whole Wheats should be no trouble for you. If you've
never kneaded before, see pp. 52–53.

When breads are made with half whole wheat and
half white flour—so many whole wheats in cookbooks are
just that, which is why I call my favorite bread "100
Percent"—they have some qualities of both. For example,
Tan French Bread will be not quite as high as the white,
but the crust will be just as crunchy and the flavor better!

100 PERCENT WHOLE WHEAT BREAD

I call this bread 100 Percent Whole Wheat Bread, but
actually it might be called 100 Percent Whole Wheat
Bread II as there are three 100 percent whole wheat
breads in this book: Dark Whole Wheat Raisin Method
Bread back in Chapter 1, this one, and Rich Whole Wheat,
which follows.

This is a water bread, and like any water bread will
dry out in a few days. But because of the preservative
power of the honey in it, it never *tastes* stale and resists
mold like crazy. I've eaten this bread after it has been
around the house for weeks, and though dry, the dryness
is like cold toast, not like stale bread—tasty and crunchy.

This recipe makes three moderate-sized loaves, either
standing free on baking sheets, or in pans. Since I often
bake more than one batch of bread at a time, I prefer

the pans, for convenience; but one gets a feeling of virtu-
osity from free-standing whole wheat loaves: the choice
is yours. But for sandwiches, use pans: the loaves can
only rise up, not out.

For all us calorie counters, this is the second-lowest
calorie bread in the book.

100 PERCENT WHOLE WHEAT BREAD

For the Dough:
  2 tbsp. active dry yeast
  ¼ cup honey
  1 tbsp. sea salt
  3 cups hot water
  6½–7½ cups whole wheat flour
For Greasing:
  melted margarine or butter
Equipment:
  large mixing bowl, mixing spoon or whisk, kneading
  board, 3 baking pans 8″ × 4″ × 2″ (or 2 baking sheets)

Mixing

Into a large mixing bowl measure **2 tablespoons of yeast,
¼ cup of honey, 1 tablespoon of salt,** and **3 cups of hot
tap water.** Stir to dissolve the salt.

Add the **first 4 cups of flour,** 2 cups at a time, wetting
thoroughly before continuing.

Mix a **fifth cup of flour** into the bowl and work in.

Spread a **sixth cup of flour** on your kneading board
and scrape the batter onto the board. Knead in.

Add another ½ **cup of flour** to the board, and knead in.

Use as much of another cup as you require for good
cohesion (lift the dough ball in one hand, palm down) and
to make the dough stop sticking to the board.

When you have worked in enough flour, knead for
an easy 15 minutes—or a vigorous 10 minutes. To keep
the dough from sticking again during this kneading, you
are entitled to flour the board lightly, even after you have
"enough" flour in.

When those characteristic light wrinkles appear on
the surface of the dough, it's ready. (If you aren't sure,
knead for another 5 minutes. The first time you do this
bread, do be sure you've kneaded enough.) Drip a few

drops of oil (or melted butter or margarine) into your
mixing bowl (no need to wash it first) and drop in the
dough ball. Turn the dough over a few times to oil all
sides. Cover with a wet, hot, clean towel, and put in a
warm, draft-free place to rise.

First Rise

On a warm day this rise should take about an hour,
though don't be surprised if it's more. This is whole wheat
flour, remember, and heavier than white.

At any rate, don't count on a specific timing for the
rise—use the finger test (see p. 54).

Shaping the Loaves

When ready, punch down and knead gently for a minute
to get out the larger air bubbles.

Divide the dough into three equal parts and shape
into three loaves. At this stage, if you opt to, you can
knead in grated orange rind or raisins (see Options).

Grease three 8″ × 4″ × 2″ baking pans (that's the
size of those disposable pans—but don't dispose of them;
they're good for many re-usings).

To make the loaves you can flatten and then roll up
the dough (as on pp. 62–63) and use that karate chop for
smoothing the ends (see p. 69)—or you can just shape
into loaf shapes as best you can. Just be sure that any
seam is on the bottom.

Fit the loaves into the pans (you can give them a
little patting here to even them off—you'll get a more
even rise that way; that is, your loaf won't hump as much
in the middle if the top is flat to begin with).

If you wish to use baking sheets to get free-standing
loaves, use two sheets and shape the dough into the same
three loaves. But once you've arrived at a shape, *don't*
even it out. Free-standing loaves are supposed to have
fat middles and tapered ends.

Rising the Loaves

This second rise can be more trouble than the first. Often,
where you have room for a bowl of dough in that warm

place, you don't have room for three loaf pans or two
baking sheets. Be sure you've read Rising Dough, pp. 19–
21. This bread is well-suited to on-top-of-the-oven rising,
because it doesn't care whether it goes into a hot or a cold
oven.

At any rate, once the dough is in the pans, re-cover
with the same towel (now barely damp), and put in a
very warm, draft-free place to rise for about half the
time of the first rise.

Baking

The loaves will rise *well above* the rim of your pans by
the time they are ready for baking.

Bake in a moderate oven, 350°–375°, for about 40
minutes.

Make certain your breads test done before you pull
them from the oven.

If the bread tests undone, but the crust shows signs
of scorching, shut the oven off and allow the bread to
stay there for another 5 or 10 minutes *with the flame off.*

Cool on a wire rack and by all means eat hot.

Options

☞ For lots of added iron, you can change the
honey in this, and most breads, to **blackstrap molasses.**
This gives you a darker colored bread with more vitamins
and minerals—but the molasses has no preservative
power. Only honey has that magic something. Maybe
you'd like to try half honey, half molasses?

☞ For an extra little zing to the taste of this
bread, add the **grated peel of half an orange,** kneading it
in well when you shape the loaves. If you're out of
oranges try some lemon peel.

☞ My husband is crazy for **raisins.** We use a big
juicy kind called Manukka (or Manoukka), which we get
from a health food store where they are sold as unsprayed
and unsulfured. I use a full cup of raisins for the batch,
but if you are only mildly fond of raisins, you might
start with ½ cup.

☞ Add **1 cup of skim milk powder** (½ cup of the
non-instant) for a little calcium.

☞ For a whole batch of other options, see the end of the next bread.

---

100 PERCENT WHOLE WHEAT BREAD—SUMMARY

A. 2 tbsp. active dry yeast   B. 6½–7½ cups whole wheat
   ¼ cup honey   flour
   1 tbsp. sea salt
   3 cups hot water

Combine A into a large bowl and mix.

Combine the first 5 cups of B, 2 cups at a time.

Spread another cup (#6) on the kneading board, and scrape batter onto the board. Knead in.

Add another ½ cup to the board and knead in.

Add more as required (up to 1 more cup).

Knead for another 15 minutes.

Drip a few drops of oil into the same bowl. Oil the dough.

Cover with a clean, hot wet towel and put to rise in a warm place.

Finger-test.

Punch down and knead gently for a minute.

Shape into three loaves.

Grease three 8″ × 4″ × 2″ baking pans, drop loaves in, re-cover with the same towel, and rise again in a warm place.

Bake in a moderate oven (350°–375°) for about 40 minutes.

Test. Cool on a wire rack and serve hot.

RICH WHOLE WHEAT BREAD

This, too, is a 100 percent whole wheat bread.

It's easy enough to see why we call this Rich Whole Wheat. It has lots of eggs, milk, oil—and the calories that go with them. But what a delicious and healthful way to get those calories.

Unlike the previous bread, this one will keep—it may not last, but if it lasts, it will keep.

Near the end of the chapter, we'll discuss a lot of healthful substitutions and additions for the recipe. So don't skip the Options, they're really important to this chapter.

Be sure you use a large mixing bowl for this bread, as the dough will climb right out of it in the rising. Forewarned is forearmed—and it's messy cleaning up dough from around your pilot light. I know.

If you are beginning with Rich Whole Wheat, be sure you take a few minutes to read what was said about kneading whole wheat dough on pp. 74–75.

RICH WHOLE WHEAT BREAD

For the Dough:
  2 tbsp. active dry yeast
  1 tbsp. sea salt
  $\frac{1}{4}$ cup vegetable oil
  $\frac{1}{4}$ cup honey
  $2\frac{1}{2}$ cups hot water
  1 cup skim milk powder
  2 cups whole wheat flour
  3 large eggs
  6–7 more cups whole wheat flour
For Greasing:
  melted margarine or butter
Equipment:
  large mixing bowl, mixing spoon or whisk, kneading board, 3 baking pans $8\frac{1}{2}'' \times 4\frac{1}{2}'' \times 2\frac{1}{2}''$

Mixing

Into a large mixing bowl measure **2 tablespoons of yeast, 1 tablespoon of salt,** and (measured in the same cup) $\frac{1}{4}$ **cup of oil** and $\frac{1}{4}$ **cup of honey.**

Add $2\frac{1}{2}$ **cups of hot tap water** and stir briefly.

Mix in **1 cup of instant skim milk powder** (or $\frac{2}{3}$ cup of non-instant).

Add **2 cups of whole wheat flour** and stir until the batter is fairly smooth. (This 2 cups of flour will help you mix the eggs into the batter more easily.)

Mix in **3 large eggs,** at room temperature. (See p. 15 and p. 19.)

Add the next **5 cups of flour,** 2 cups at a time, making certain it's all wetted before going on to the next 2 cups.

Dump another **cup of flour** (#8) onto the board and scrape the batter over it. Knead in, adding small amounts of flour as required, until the dough stops sticking.

Knead for another 10–15 minutes. The oil in this dough makes it easier to handle than 100 Percent Whole Wheat.

First Rise

When the dough is kneaded (you will see those satiny wrinkles), pour a few drops of oil back into the original bowl, drop the dough ball in, turning it over a few times to make sure it's all oiled, cover with a clean, hot, *wet* towel, and put in a warm, draft-free place to rise (about an hour or a little more).

Finger-test (see p. 54).

Rising the Loaves

If, after testing, that hole doesn't fill, punch the dough down, knead it for a moment to get rid of some of the bubbles, divide into three pieces, and shape into loaves.

By this time the dough feels absolutely lovely, is very easy to handle, and wouldn't dream of sticking to anything.

Grease three $8\frac{1}{2}'' \times 4\frac{1}{2}'' \times 2\frac{1}{2}''$ baking pans and drop the loaves in. Use your fingers to level off the loaves.

Re-cover with that same towel, and put into a very warm place to rise again (about $\frac{1}{2}$ hour).

Baking

When the loaves are well risen, put them to bake in a moderate oven (350°–375°) for about 40 minutes.

Test with a clean knife for doneness. These are fairly high loaves, so, inserting through the bottom crust, make sure your knife goes almost to the top, without piercing the top crust.

Cool on a wire rack.

This bread will keep, so don't be afraid to make more loaves than you can use today and tomorrow.

Options

SUBSTITUTIONS

In these whole wheat recipes you are entitled to a full cup of substitutions, though you can use less. By this, I don't mean additions, like raisins or sunflower seeds, I mean *substitutions*. As in earlier recipes we have substituted wheat germ for white flour to make a white recipe healthier, here we can substitute various flours to make these whole wheat breads healthier and more varied.

If you wish to juggle the various flours around, using ½ cup of this and ¼ cup each of this and that—go ahead. The only limit is your imagination—and that 1 cup. (Actually, if you don't mind heavy bread, you can substitute even more than 1 cup.)

☞ You can make "super-bread" by substituting **wheat germ** for 1 cup of whole wheat flour.

☞ **Soy flour or meal** is highly recommended by many nutritionists, because it has so much good protein and lecithin. If you want to use more than 1 cup of soy flour, you have to compensate by including some **gluten flour** to make up for the lack of gluten in the soy: for example, 2 cups of soy and 1 cup of gluten flour as a substitute for 3 cups of whole wheat.

☞ Also recommended are such coarse grains as **cracked wheat, wheat grits, rye meal,** and **cornmeal.** (For rye–whole wheat combinations, see Pumpernickel, Sour Pumpernickel, and Snack Breads.)

☞ Certain healthful cereals such as **Granola, Familia,** or **Wheat Germ Cereal** (though they contain sugar) are acceptable substitutions. (We used to breakfast on such cereals extensively—and expensively—but since we've been baking our own whole grain breads, we make our own "bread-cereal": whole grain bread crumbled and tossed with a little raw wheat germ, cut-up apple and/or other fresh fruit, seeds, a bit of dried fruit—add milk and it's great. And no sugar.)

☞ **Buckwheat flour** has a strong flavor, but you might want to experiment with small amounts.

☞ By all means try some **bran** or **rice polish**— these outer coverings are rich in B vitamins.

☞ **Millet** is worth trying, and **oatmeal,** while not as healthful as whole wheat, is good for variety.

☞   Other possible substitutes, if you can find
them, are: **brown rice flour, barley flour, sunflower seed
meal, flaxseed meal,** and **carob powder** (this last is a substitute for chocolate that kids will accept).

☞   So-called **eating yeast** fits in here, too, and is
good, healthful stuff. Until you know how you like its
strong flavor—it's an acquired taste—start out with a
small amount—substituting, say, 3 tablespoons for 3 tablespoons of flour for the entire batch. It is also called
torula yeast or brewer's yeast. Unlike the yeast we bake
with, it is not alive when you buy it.

☞   And let's not forget the substitution of **blackstrap molasses** for all or part of the honey, as we discussed with 100 Percent Whole Wheat Bread.

ADDITIONS

☞   As with the last bread, knead the **grated rind
of half a citrus fruit** into the loaves.

☞   Knead in **1 cup of raisins,** as you shape the
loaves, or ½ cup to 1 cup of any **dried fruit, nut,** or **seed**
combination that strikes your fancy or your palate. Sunflower seeds combined with raisins are great for this
bread.

☞   For a crazy crunch, you might try adding ½ cup
of well-drained **bean sprouts** (home-sprouted, I hope—
they are infinitely superior to canned).

☞   For a pleasantly shiny **glaze,** brush the hot
crust with melted butter or margarine as soon as the
bread is out of the oven.

The possible combinations are vast in number, and
can all add to the interest or, more important, the health-
fulness of this already nutritious bread.

WHOLE WHEAT ROLLS

This Rich Whole Wheat dough is a natural for Whole
Wheat Rolls, because the things that make it rich also
make it easy to handle. But the 100 Percent Whole Wheat
Bread dough (or any kneaded dough in the book) can
also be used for these rolls. (If you are using a water
dough, keeping it in the fridge for a day or so will make
it easier to handle.)

These rolls are very simple to shape; the same recipe that makes three loaves of Rich Whole Wheat Bread makes about two dozen Whole Wheat Rolls. But what I like to do is bake two loaves of bread and put a third of the kneaded dough aside in the fridge until the loaves are gone, and then bake up the rolls (or vice versa). This dough will keep quite well in the fridge for 2 weeks.

To make these rolls, shape the dough into hockey puck rounds, about 1 inch by 3 inches, and lay the rounds on a greased baking sheet (if you make up the whole batch, you'll need two sheets) so that they don't touch.

Now, take a metal-handled knife, and press the handle firmly and evenly all the way across each roll, pressing almost down to the sheet, and wiggle it. This will divide the rolls almost in half. Don't fold the rounds.

Shaping Whole Wheat Rolls

Cover with a clean towel and put into a very warm place to rise for half an hour. They won't rise much, but that's all right.

Mix a thin **egg-yolk glaze** (1 egg yolk stirred with 1 tablespoon of water) and brush over the surface.

Sprinkle with **poppy seeds** while the glaze is still wet.

Bake in the same moderate oven for 20 minutes. The tops will turn a lovely golden brown.

These take so little time and planning (especially if you've reserved a part of the dough from your other baking) that they are great dinner rolls, coming to the table right from the oven, to be eaten at once. Rolls tend to get stale faster than a bread of the same dough, but these rich dough rolls keep quite well.

If you are using dough that's been kept in the fridge, do take it out a couple of hours ahead of time to allow it to come to room temperature. Or if you haven't time, not to worry—just allow a few more minutes for that rise in a warm place.

Remember, any of the options we offered for the bread hold for these rolls, too.

RICH WHOLE WHEAT BREAD—SUMMARY

A. 2 tbsp. active dry yeast
1 tbsp. sea salt

B. ¼ cup vegetable oil
¼ cup honey

C. 2½ cups hot water

D. 1 cup skim milk powder

E. 2 cups whole wheat flour

F. 3 eggs

G. 6–7 more cups whole wheat flour

Into a large mixing bowl measure A.
Measure B into a cup and stir into A.
Add C and stir.
Mix in D.
Add E, and mix until fairly smooth.
Stir in F.
Add 5 cups of G, 2 cups at a time.
Dump another cup (no. 8) over the kneading board, and scrape batter out onto board. Knead in.
Add as much of ninth cup as necessary to stop dough from sticking.
Knead for another 10–15 minutes.
Oil the ball in the bowl, cover with a clean, wet towel, and put to rise in a very warm, draft-free place.
Finger-test.
When risen, punch down and shape into three loaves. (At this point make any seed, fruit, or nut additions.)
Grease three 8½″ × 4½″ × 2½″ baking pans.
Put loaves into pans, cover again with wet towel, and put again to rise in a very warm place.
Bake for about 40 minutes at 350°–375°.
Knife-test.
Cool on a wire rack.
Eat hot—but any left over will keep.

5

Sourdough—
Trapping
the
Wild
Yeast

What with television, the word "sourdough" must be familiar to everyone—the sourdoughs were Alaskan prospectors.

They were called sourdoughs because while prospecting they carried around with them a bit of homemade yeast (a "sourdough starter") which had begun life as a mixture of soured milk and flour and which they had, no doubt, bought from or been gifted by some earlier sourdough. They would carry this starter (mostly dry from the addition of flour) wrapped up inside their packs or inside their shirts to keep it from freezing. When they camped they would mix it with water and flour to make dough, saving a bit of it as a starter for next day's camp. Thus, even though no supermarket was around with prepackaged yeast, they were able to have yeast-risen bread—that is, Sourdough Bread.

On the West Coast and in Alaska, it's claimed that some of those original strains of sourdough (which may have come over with the Russian settlers of Alaska) are still alive. But you'll find sourdough breads on the East Coast and in-between coasts, too. So-called sour ryes incorporate sourdough, so do some English Muffins, and the various sourdough breads labeled as such.

BORNE FREE

What is sourdough? Actually, it's *free yeast.*

There are in the air, all around us, microscopic organ-

isms. The three main groupings are bacteria, molds, and
yeasts. Some are harmful to human beings, some are
friendly, and many are indifferent. Any of them, when they
chance upon a favorable medium, a welcoming environment, grow and multiply. (For example, yeasts like a wetter environment than molds do; if you set out something
just moist, you are likely to see the visible mold colonies
in a couple of days.)

If you can encourage wild yeast to grow in a favorable medium (such as a wet and warm mixture made
from milk and flour) they will multiply and act for you like
prepackaged yeast—with the major difference that the
taste is a "sour," winey, rich flavor which can really
turn your taste buds on.

We'll use it here in a half-dozen recipes with many
possible variations: Sourdough French (tan or wheat germ
or white), Pumpernickel, English Muffins, Sour Rye, Pan
Loaves, and Snack Breads.

It's not that these breads, with some change in the
recipes, can't be made with the same old reliable active
dry yeast; it's that Sourdough Breads are altogether something else to taste. So, for flavor, variety, and economy—
if you need justification—it's worth the bit of extra planning necessary to make Sourdough Breads.

(If you already own some sourdough starter, or have
a friend who will give you some, skip this next section
and go on to Doubling, p. 89.)

TRAPPING THE WILD YEAST

There are several ways of obtaining sourdough starter:
you can buy good strains of starter in many health food
stores or by mail from Walnut Acres, Penns Creek, Pennsylvania, or El Molino Mills, Alhambra, California; or you
can get yours the same way I got mine—by trapping the
wild yeast into a favorable medium.

I started with a cup of reconstituted powdered skim
milk. Even if you use whole milk for everything else, I
suggest you start with skim milk. It's not that it sours
more quickly (though it often seems to), it's that with
homogenized milk, because the fat molecules are so
evenly distributed, it's not as easy to *tell* when the milk
has begun to go sour.

Covering the cup of milk with a bit of cloth (only

to keep out dust and wandering bugs) I left it on my side-board for almost two days, until it smelled sour.

Once it soured, I added a cup of flour, then stirred the mixture and covered it loosely again. (Note: 1 cup of milk plus 1 cup of flour makes about 1 cup of mixture.)

Within a couple of days the mixture had begun to make bubbles (a sure sign that yeast is in residence) and had taken on a spongy look. Don't worry if the liquid separates out on top—you can stir that right back in.

If you get no bubbling action by the fifth day of your project—start over.

If you get various colored molds on top—throw it away and start over. (Probably your médium was too dry and so more inviting to wandering molds than wandering yeast.) All you've wasted is a cup of milk and a cup of flour—less than the cost of a packet of yeast.

(There are, in various cookbooks, recipes for making "sourdough" starter using tame yeast and flour and milk, or tame yeast and flour and milk and a shot of vinegar. It's not the same—it's not even close. Tame yeast is tame, and only wild yeast gives you that great sourdough flavor.)

If you bake with your new starter the first week, you may be surprised at how bland it is *that first week*. It seems that sourdough culture likes to mature for a few weeks before it hits its full flavor stride. It will raise your bread immediately, but the flavor needs maturing, at least until the second week.

DOUBLING

Now you have a cup of starter. But since most sourdough recipes call for at least a cup of starter, you have to double—unless you want to go through the process of obtaining a new culture every time you bake.

Here's how to double: to your 1 cup of starter you add 1 cup of milk and 1 cup of flour. You stir the mixture together until it's fairly uniform, then leave it out at room temperature (loosely covered) for a few hours, then, when it looks spongy, refrigerate. What you now have is 2 cups of sourdough starter.

CARE AND MAINTENANCE

I keep my sourdough starter in plastic containers in the fridge with the covers on loosely. The starter is a live and lively yeast, and it is in the nature of yeast to make bubbles. And if it goes on making bubbles (as it does) and you've put the cover on that container good and tight—something's got to give.

There is an alternative: you can keep your sourdough starter in a ceramic crock (avoid metal altogether—the chemical reactions can be unhealthy) with a strong clamp.

Whichever way you store it, it must be stored cold, otherwise the culture would soon destroy itself in its own waste products.

Even in the fridge the life processes go on, though slowly, and if you keep your starter for a month without using it, you have to divide it and double again (providing fresh food for the remaining half). You can throw away the other half, or give it to a friend, with instructions on doubling.

A friend of ours freezes his sourdough starter (an old California strain) for six months at a time—taking it out of the freezer every six months (when he hasn't baked with it) for thawing, doubling, and refreezing.

GENERAL SOURDOUGH TECHNIQUE

Sourdough breads are not quick to make. They don't require any more work or watching than other breads, but they do require more time and a little more planning.

All of the following sourdough recipes give instructions on a "first day–second day" basis. There is no magic in the passing of a night, it's just that sourdough yeast is a much slower-acting yeast, and requires about 12 hours to grow enough to use.

The first day, or early in the morning of the baking day, you put together a very *wet* mixture which, because of the bubbliness of the yeast, is known as the sponge.

Of course, if your kitchen is quite cool, the sponge could take longer than twelve hours, and if your kitchen is hot or it's the middle of a heat wave, it could take hours less.

The sponge is made with a part of the flour, the honey (or molasses), and all of the liquid. We don't put salt in the sponge because it tends to retard the yeast action.

Once the sponge is risen, which means that the wild yeast has permeated every part of the flour and liquid mixture, you add the rest of the ingredients and then knead it. This is just the opposite of the pattern you learned for other kneaded breads, where first you knead and then rise, *for sourdoughs you rise in the sponge and then knead.*

Here, again, you need extra time after shaping. Sourdough loaves generally require 2–3 hours to rise. And, if your kitchen is cold, they may require even longer.

Most of these sourdough recipes call for the use of baking soda (bicarbonate of soda). The soda provides a bit of extra rising help. The starter is acid, the soda is base, and the chemical reaction when these two meet is to make bubbles as the starter neutralizes the soda.

But never use more than the amount of baking soda called for in my sourdough recipes. Any unneutralized soda will leave an unpleasant metallic taste, and, what's worse, will destroy some of the body's vitamins.

If you wish, the soda can be omitted altogether, leaving you with a slightly lower bread and a slightly more acid flavor.

SOURDOUGH FRENCH BREAD

Remember that basic water bread (our convertible French-Portuguese-Cuban Bread) back in Chapter 3? Well, here it is again, just as lovely to look at and with as fine a texture, but with a delicious difference in flavor. I won't describe the difference here; it's better if you make up your own superlatives.

I recommend quite strongly the substitution of wheat germ for some of the white in this bread (see p. 95), but you may prefer Sourdough Tan French (p. 95), which is quite good, too. It's a matter of taste.

Don't expect Sourdough French to rise quite as high as did our earlier French Bread. The sourdough yeast doesn't have as big a rising "kick" as does active dry yeast. But the difference is quite small.

SOURDOUGH FRENCH BREAD

The First Day:
    1 cup starter
    1½ cups hot tap water
    1 tbsp. honey
    3½ cups unbleached white flour
The Second Day:
    1 tbsp. sea salt
    ½ tsp. baking soda
    2–3 cups unbleached white flour (only enough to knead comfortably)
For Greasing:
    melted butter or margarine
    sprinkling of cornmeal
Equipment:
    mixing bowl and spoon, kneading board, 2 large baking sheets, sharp knife

The First Day

Prepare your sponge by mixing together in a large bowl: **1 cup of starter, 1½ cups of hot water, 1 tablespoon of honey,** and **2 cups of flour.** Stir until the mixture is smooth, then add **1½ cups of flour** and stir again.

The sponge will not be creamy smooth at this time, and you don't have to try to make it so. Just make sure that all the flour is mixed in.

Cover with wax paper or plastic and a clean towel and put aside, out of drafts and *at room temperature,* until tomorrow morning—at least 12 hours. (The towel provides a tent to keep drafts off the top of the bowl.)

The Second Day

When you take the towel off, you may find that the sponge has risen to the paper and stuck to it. No worry, just scrape off the sticking batter and throw it back into the bowl. Or you may find that a crust has formed over the surface. This is quite normal; all you have to do is stir the crust under, and it will soon disappear into the batter.

But, crust or no, stir down the batter to about its original size.

Sprinkle over the surface of the stirred batter **1 tablespoon of salt** and a **scant ½ teaspoon of baking soda,** and mix these in with your spoon—even though the batter may be a little resistant to stirring.

Add ½ cup of flour to the bowl and stir it in until most of it disappears.

Dump 1 cup of flour onto the center of your kneading board and spread it around a bit.

Empty the bowl onto this flour. (Do scrape out the bowl when you empty it.) Pour another ½ cup of flour over the top of the dough, and you're ready to begin kneading. (If you've never kneaded before, see pp. 52–53.)

Of course, the dough will be very wet to begin with, offering little more resistance than jellied consommé, but as you work in more flour, you'll approach something that feels like dough.

At this point your judgment comes in. You have used, so far, 5½ cups of flour—the minimum for this kind of bread. Is this enough? Or should you add another cup, up to the maximum? (Or, conceivably, beyond it?)

There is no *perfect* amount of flour. Some bakers like a "wet" dough which they feel produces lighter bread— others prefer a dry dough to get a solid, substantial bread. The amount of flour must depend on your feel for the dough, on that particular day, for that particular bread— and it's hard to be wrong.

When you've added as much flour as you think is necessary, knead the bread well for 10 minutes.

Even though you have "enough" flour in your dough, it may be necessary to add sprinklings of flour to the board to keep it from sticking while you knead. Don't think of this as adding to the total—it should be a very thin layer.

Shaping the Loaves

When those "wrinkles" appear (see p. 53), knead for a few more minutes to make sure, then leave the dough on your board and grease two large baking sheets.

Sprinkle the sheets with a small amount of **cornmeal** (this is to help with bottom crust), and then shake the sheets from side to side to distribute the meal uniformly.

Cut the dough in half, and roll each half on the board to shape a long, thin loaf (if you start rolling with your hands in the middle and move toward the ends, you're more likely to come up with something even). At this

point the loaf should be about 1½–2 inches thick and long
enough to stretch diagonally across your baking sheet.

If you don't have two sheets that are large enough,
divide the dough into three pieces and shape three loaves,
each about 1½ inches thick (put two on one sheet, one on
another), and long enough to stretch the length of the
sheet.

Cover with a clean towel or two, to keep the loaves
both warm and clean, and put in a warm place to rise (see
Rising Dough, pp. 19–21) for 2–3 hours—or until the loaves
are *considerably* larger.

Frenching

Now we come to those things that make this "French"
Bread.

When the loaves have risen sufficiently, put a couple
of cups of water on to boil; this will eventually make
steam in the oven.

Meanwhile, spray the loaves with water. You can use
any kind of sprayer or sprinkler (though if you use a flit
gun, watch out for rust), or you can sprinkle with your
fingers, or brush on the water with a pastry brush (so
long as you are very gentle). And don't be stingy—it's this
water that gives the loaves a good crust.

Now it's time for surgery. With a very sharp or serrated knife, slash diagonally, three or four slashes, to a
depth of about one-eighth inch. Be very careful not to slash
too hard. If you do, the loaf will fall, and you'll have to
wait for it to rise again—very frustrating. If you want
to slash *before* spraying, go right ahead—it won't matter.
And be sure you do slash diagonally, not lengthwise—that
would spread the loaf wide; we want it to rise *up*.

Baking

French Bread—this or any other made in a home oven—
must go into a cold oven (that is, under 200°: if you've
been using it, let the oven cool down to this temperature).
Pour the water you've been boiling into a pan and place it
somewhere in the oven, out of the way of the bread.

Now light your oven. This bread will bake, eventually,
at 350°–375°, and you can set your oven for that (medium-
low). I say "eventually" because you will have to open the

oven after 5 minutes of baking to spray the loaves again, and 5 minutes after that to spray for a third time, and this repeated opening and spraying cools the oven down.

Even with the spraying and opening of the oven, this bread will bake in 30–35 minutes, and take on a beautiful golden tan.

But remember, ovens vary, and yours and mine are sure to have different hot spots. Know your own oven and its baking times. Don't assume a loaf is done because it looks done—test (see pp. 21–23).

If these loaves test done, put them onto a cooling rack for a few minutes before you tear one open.

Options

☞ The main option you have with this bread is to make it a lot healthier. While unbleached flour contains more vitamins than bleached, it is still nutritionally scant pickings. So I recommend the substitution of ½ **cup of raw wheat germ** for ½ cup of the flour. Make this substitution the second day, adding the wheat germ instead of the last ½ cup of flour that goes into the bowl. We routinely make all our white breads with raw wheat germ.

☞ Sourdough Tan French is excellent. Substitute **whole wheat flour** for all the flour used the second day. Actually, you can substitute whole wheat for half the total white flour used in the recipe—which means you would use some whole wheat in making up the sponge the first day.

☞ If you would like a crust of a deeper color, use an **egg-white glaze.** In the last 5 or 10 minutes of baking, spread the surface of the loaves with stirred egg white (mixed with a teaspoon of water if it feels too thick to handle easily) and then sprinkle the tops of the loaves with **sesame seeds.**

SOURDOUGH FRENCH BREAD—SUMMARY

A. 1 cup starter
   1½ cups hot water
   1 tbsp. honey
   3½ cups flour

B. 1 tbsp. sea salt
   ½ tsp. baking soda

C. 2–3 cups flour

The night before (or early the same day) combine A into a large bowl.

At least 12 hours later, stir down and sprinkle B over the surface of the sponge and mix in.

Stir in ½ cup of C.

Flour the board with 1 cup of C, and knead in as much of the remainder as required to make a comfortable dough.

Knead for 10 minutes.

Shape into two long loaves and place on greased and cornmealed baking sheets. Cover with a clean towel, and put aside to rise for 2–3 hours.

When well risen, slash the loaves and spray them with water.

Put a pan of boiling water into the bottom of the oven.

Put the loaves into a cold oven and bake for 30–35 minutes at 350°–375°.

Spray again with water after 5 and after 10 minutes of baking. Test for doneness, cool briefly on a wire rack, and serve hot.

SOURDOUGH PAN LOAVES

Notice that in this bread the wheat germ is not an "option" but one of the regular ingredients: it's the wheat germ that makes this bread as tasty as it is.

This is a moister recipe than most of the Sourdough Breads, and therefore makes for a livelier batter, so be sure to use a bowl large enough both to hold the mixture as it expands and for kneading in later on. For this bread you don't even require a kneading board—*you'll knead it right in the bowl.* This will enable you to have a moister dough than is possible on a board (where you must keep adding flour to keep the dough from sticking), and so a lighter bread.

As the name states, these are not free-standing loaves but loaves made in a pan. I use a pan 9½″ × 5½″, and get two large loaves out of the recipe. They rise well, so if you want to use smaller pans, divide the dough into *three* loaves.

The dough you finish with is much softer and somewhat wetter and stickier than most you've been used to (that's why it's in the pan), so don't try to make this one conform—leave it soft and wet, or you'll wind up with a heavy bread.

This is a coarse, country-looking loaf, whose pan shape makes it excellent for sandwiches, while the combination of sourdough and wheat germ gives it a full, hearty flavor.

SOURDOUGH PAN LOAVES

The First Day:
  1 cup starter
  2½ cups water
  2 tbsp. honey
  5 cups unbleached white flour
The Second Day:
  3 tbsp. vegetable oil
  1 tbsp. sea salt
  1 scant tsp. baking soda
  1 cup raw wheat germ
  1½–2 cups unbleached white flour
For Greasing:
  melted butter or margarine
Equipment:
  large mixing bowl, mixing spoon, 2 loaf pans 9½″ × 5½″

The First Day

In your bowl, mix together the **starter,** the **water,** and the **honey** until fairly smooth. Then stir in the **flour** 2 cups at a time.

Cover with a clean towel and put aside in a draft-free place to rise at room temperature overnight or for 12 hours. (Actually, what you're doing here is giving the yeast of the starter a chance to "sour" as much of the flour as possible. If you were to put in all the flour to begin with, the sponge would be too dry; yeast grows best in a wet environment.)

The Second Day

Stir the sponge down, mixing in the crust that has most likely formed.

To the sponge add **3 tablespoons of oil, 1 tablespoon**

of salt, and a scant teaspoon of baking soda, and stir in until blended.

Add 1 cup of raw wheat germ (the toasted will do if you can't get raw, but it's more expensive and poorer in vitamins) and mix in.

Add in the flour, ½ cup at a time, kneading in all the visible flour before adding the next ½ cup.

Unless the dough is uncomfortably wet, stop after 1½ cups of flour. At any rate, only when the day is very humid are you likely to want more than 2 cups (a *total* of 7 cups of flour).

Kneading

Knead in the bowl for 10 minutes or so.

If you've never kneaded in a bowl, the technique is even simpler than board kneading. Just make sure the bowl is in a comfortable and relatively secure position at about arm's length, and then press the dough with your closed fist, then squeeze it with your fingers.

This bread will never stop sticking to your hands as you knead—though as time goes on it will tend to stick less. However, the dough ball will show cohesion when you pick it up and let it hang from your hand.

If you're not sure, knead some more.

Shaping the Loaves

Grease two 9½″ × 5½″ × 2¾″ loaf pans.

Divide the dough into two equal portions and form each half into the rough shape of a loaf.

Drop each half into a pan, and, with your fingers, even off the loaves so that the tops are fairly level. Any bumps or peaks will tend to stay as they are.

Rising the Loaves

Cover the loaves with a clean towel and put to rise in a warm place for 1½–2 hours. The dough will rise to almost fill the pan.

Remember, sourdough is slower to rise than tame yeast doughs, and rising time will depend a great deal on the vitality of your starter.

Baking

When the dough about fills the pans, put them into your oven and bake for about 45 minutes at 360°–400°, medium-high.

When done, turn out onto a cooling rack and let cool for several minutes before slicing.

This is a bread with a grand crust—you'll enjoy it.

Options

☞ Substituting **1 cup of cornmeal** for the wheat germ gives a satisfying crunchiness—for those who like a bit of backtalk in their bread. For those who like crunchiness and wheat germ, use ½ cup of cornmeal and ½ cup of wheat germ.

☞ Substituting **1 cup of oatmeal** for the wheat germ gives you Oatmeal Sourdough Bread.

☞ Brushing the tops of the loaves with **melted butter** or **margarine** as soon as they are turned onto the cooling rack will give you a shiny glaze. But for my money that's strictly Madison Avenue. There is no taste difference.

SOURDOUGH PAN LOAVES—SUMMARY

A. 1 cup starter   B. 3 tbsp. oil
   2½ cups water   1 tbsp. sea salt
   2 tbsp. honey   1 scant tsp. baking soda
   5 cups flour

C. 1 cup raw wheat germ

D. 1½–2 cups flour

The first day make your sponge by combining A into a large bowl until smooth. Cover and put into a draft-free place to rise.

The second day stir down the sponge and work in B.

Add C and mix until completely wetted.

Add D to the bowl a ½ cup at a time.

Knead in the bowl for about 10 minutes.

Grease two 9½″ × 5½″ × 2¾″ pans with melted butter or margarine.

Divide the dough in half, shape into loaves, and put in pans.

Cover and allow to rise in a warm place for 1½–2 hours. The dough will rise to about fill the pans.

Bake for about 45 minutes at 360°–400°.

Turn out, test, and cool.

SOURDOUGH ENGLISH MUFFINS

This one's really kicky—you can get the whole family in on it.

I understand that you can't get English Muffins in England—there you have to ask for scones (to rhyme with "on"). But scones are heavy, and these Sourdough English Muffins are as light as you could wish for; and they taste better than the commercial variety.

Apparently, these muffins are called "English" because they are fried in a griddle on top of the stove, which is the way the English cook everything. Whatever the etymology, this is a bread cooked *without the oven*— what a break for the summer months!

In making English Muffins, pay special attention to the size of the flame under your griddle. The directions call for a low flame, and when I say *low* I mean *simmering low*. It will take an extra 5 minutes for the griddle to preheat, but once it's heated, the muffins will take only 8–10 minutes per batch to cook (4–5 minutes per side). This will give you a muffin still moist but done. But, as with any bread, there is only one ultimate test—break one open and look at it.

I find it very easy to cook four muffins at a time in the center of my 10-inch square griddle. With an electric frying pan you ought to be able to do better than that, since you'll have even heat in the corners of the pan. With an ordinary frying pan (a last resort) you're probably back to four at a time.

Butter the griddle only once (and that lightly), before putting up the first batch.

The cornmeal that you sprinkle on the wax paper and over the rising muffins serves two purposes: it makes the raw muffins easier to handle, that is, less likely to stick to the paper; and it gives them, after cooking, a bit more crunchiness, which is very much to the good.

This, like all sourdough breads, has to be started the night before, so try to get that "I-want-English-Muffins-for-breakfast!" feeling before you go to bed.

This recipe makes about 30 muffins, if you use a 3-inch cutter. If that's too many for your family, reserve a third or half of the kneaded dough and put the rest in the fridge for tomorrow—or next week. When you want your next batch of muffins, just let the dough come to room temperature before rolling it out. Or, you can cook up the whole batch, freeze as many as you like, and take them out of the freezer and toast them when they're wanted.

SOURDOUGH ENGLISH MUFFINS

The Night Before:
  1 cup starter
  2 tbsp. honey
  2 cups reconstituted skim milk (or whole milk)
  4 cups unbleached white flour
The Morning After:
  1 scant tsp. baking soda
  2 tsp. sea salt
  1–2 cups unbleached white flour
  cornmeal for sprinkling
Equipment:
  mixing bowl and spoon, kneading board, wax paper, rolling pin, 3" cutter (an empty tuna-fish can will do), griddle (or frying pan), pancake turner

The Night Before

Mix together **1 cup of sourdough starter, 2 tablespoons of honey,** and **2 cups of reconstituted skim milk** (if you're making these for kids, use whole milk). Just swish these together in the mixing bowl until they are smooth.

Add **4 cups of flour,** 2 cups at a time, and mix in. There's no need for any gluten development now, so do not whip—just get all the flour thoroughly wet.

Cover with a clean towel and leave at room temperature in a draft-free place.

The Morning After

Uncover your mixture and stir it down (it will have risen considerably). If it has risen too high and fallen, no problem, just stir it down the rest of the way.

Sprinkle a **scant teaspoon of baking soda** and **2 teaspoons of salt** over the surface of the dough and work in.

Flour your board with a **cup of flour,** and dump the mixture onto your kneading board.

You'll want to knead in this 1 cup of flour or more (up to 2 cups), until the dough is medium stiff—stiff enough to roll out.

Once you have enough flour in (when the dough no longer sticks to your hands), give it a 5-minute kneading—that's enough because in this dough we're not all that concerned with gluten development since the muffins are so small.

Up to this point you've been doing fairly familiar things with your dough. In fact, you could throw away the rest of the recipe, knead for another 5 or 10 minutes, divide into loaves, and make Sourdough Sandwich Bread (see p. 104).

Shaping the Muffins

Bring on the kiddies.

Flour the board lightly and roll the dough out to a half-inch thickness. (I use a rolling pin, but I begin by patting the dough somewhat flat.) Try to get the dough pretty close to a half inch; thinner and it will make too many muffins; thicker and the muffins will require more time to cook—coming close to burning on the outside and barely done inside.

Take a 3-inch round cutter (there's really no reason why you can't use a larger cutter, or a square or oblong cutter—or any shape you wish; it's just that commercially made muffins are cut about 3 inches and so that's what most people are used to) and cut as many rounds as you can from your rolled-out dough.

Spread wax paper on a couple of baking sheets or platters or trays and sprinkle with **cornmeal.**

As you cut out each round, lay it on the cornmealed wax paper—don't let the raw muffins touch each other, they'll stick.

When you've cut out all the rounds possible the first time through, squeeze the remaining dough into a ball, and roll it out again into that same half-inch thickness. Again cut your 3-inch rounds. And so on, until you've used up all your dough, and the muffins are laid out neatly on the wax paper.

Now sprinkle some additional cornmeal over the tops —not a lot.

Cover with a clean towel and put into a warm place to rise for about a half hour—that is, a half hour from when the *first* round was cut out. If your children are cutting the muffins and doing it slowly, the first set may be ready to cook by the time the last set is cut out. If, after half an hour, you don't see any rising, your place is probably too cool, so re-cover and let them go another half hour.

Cooking

When the muffins are ready to cook (don't test them, just look: they will be about three quarters of an inch thick now), preheat your griddle by putting it over a *low* flame for about 5 minutes, or until a drop of water will skitter on it.

I grease my griddle before preheating, only once for the whole batch. If you're using a frying pan, you'll need more greasing as you work.

Use a pancake turner or a spatula to loosen the muffins from the wax paper and to transport them to the griddle. Do not raise your flame. Try to keep them from touching each other on the griddle until they've cooked for a couple of minutes.

Cook on each side for 4–5 minutes, depending on the thickness of the raw rounds. If you managed to roll them a half inch thick, 4 minutes per side should do; thicker muffins require 5 minutes per side.

Here, in cooking, timing, and turning the muffins, is another perfect opportunity to use my no-work method— I give my husband the stopwatch and let him sit at the stove and do it. But even a large child would do.

These muffins are turned only once, so be sure to let them get done on that first side.

If your muffins rise to look like baseballs, you may flatten them *slightly* by pressing *gently* with your pancake turner when you turn them over to do the second side. This squares off the shoulders a bit; but don't lean on them.

By all means test the first muffin to come off the griddle. Tear it open and look for raw spots, then taste it. Remember, though, these are fresh and not yet toasted— the way that most of us are used to eating English Muffins. If you want to, split and grill them right now.

Options

☞ To make these healthier, as well as even more delicious, you can substitute ½ cup of wheat germ for white flour (in which case you can knead it in with the last of the flour), or you can substitute whole wheat flour for the last 1–2 cups of flour in the recipe.

☞ If you want to make Sourdough Sandwich Bread, divide the kneaded dough and put it into two greased 8-inch pans, and allow to rise for about an hour in a very warm place. Then bake in a moderate oven (about 350°), for 40 minutes.

SOURDOUGH ENGLISH MUFFINS—SUMMARY

A. 1 cup starter
   2 tbsp. honey
   2 cups reconstituted
      skim (or whole) milk
   4 cups flour

B. 1 scant tsp. baking soda
   2 tsp. sea salt

C. 1–2 cups flour

The night before, combine A into a large bowl until smooth.

Cover and put into a draft-free place to rise.

The next morning stir down and mix in B.

Flour your board with 1 cup of C and dump mixture onto board. Knead in as much of C as necessary to make dough non-sticky.

Knead for 5 minutes more.

Flour board lightly and roll or pat out dough to half-inch thickness.

With a 3-inch cutter, cut rounds from the dough, re-rolling until all the dough is in rounds.

As rounds are cut, place them on cornmealed wax paper. Sprinkle lightly with cornmeal.

Cover and allow to rise in a warm place for a half hour.

Preheat griddle (simmering low) for 5 minutes.

Cook 4–5 minutes per side, turning only once.

If necessary, press gently with pancake turner on second side to even off shape.

SOUR PUMPERNICKEL

I wish I knew what magic there is in bought bread that sets the standard for what bread is supposed to look like. So many times my students tell me of having to all but force their families into that first taste of homemade bread (which, of course, is always gobbled up after the first bite) simply because it doesn't look exactly like the bread that comes from the supermarket or bakery.

Well, here's a bread that bakes up to look so much like bakery bread that you can fool anyone—up to the first bite, that is, because the taste is like nothing you get in a bakery.

"Robust" is the word that best describes Sour Pumpernickel. Pile on the strong cheese and the onions and mustard—this bread still keeps its character and flavor.

It is, of course, sour—though not as sour as some breads—with the additional fillip of the flavor of rye and whole wheat, plus the added healthiness of blackstrap molasses.

The texture of the loaf is medium-light—just right for a sandwich, as well as excellent for toasting.

For this bread we use an egg-yolk glaze about 10 minutes before the loaves are finished baking; this serves two purposes: first, it helps to give that grand final dark color that is so traditional for pumpernickel; and, second, the egg helps to hold the final sprinkling of caraway seeds.

I find this Sour Pumpernickel easier to make than the standard Pumpernickel you will make in Chapter 7. Perhaps it's because of the overnight rise, but I find the dough ready to shape into loaves with much less kneading.

SOUR PUMPERNICKEL

The First Day:
   1 cup starter
   2 cups reconstituted skim milk
   2 tbsp. blackstrap molasses
   ¼ cup vegetable oil
   1 cup unbleached white flour
   1 cup whole rye flour
   2 cups whole wheat flour
The Second Day:
   1 tbsp. sea salt
   ½ scant tsp. baking soda
   ½ cup whole rye flour
   1–1½ cups unbleached white flour
   1 tbsp. caraway seeds
For Greasing:
   melted butter or margarine
   white cornmeal for sprinkling
For Glazing:
   egg yolk
   caraway seeds
Equipment:
   large mixing bowl and spoon (or whisk), 2 baking
   sheets, pastry brush (optional)

The Night Before

Make up your sponge by combining in a large bowl **1 cup
of starter, 2 cups of reconstituted skim milk, 2 tablespoons
of blackstrap molasses, ¼ cup of vegetable oil, 1 cup of
white flour, 1 cup of rye flour,** and **2 cups of whole wheat
flour.** I find it easiest to blend the whole if I stir in the
flour 1 cup at a time. A whisk is very handy for this
session.

Stir until it's smooth, then cover with a wet towel
overnight, in a draft-free place.

The Morning After

At least 12 hours later, stir the sponge down to its original
size.

Over the surface of the sponge sprinkle **1 tablespoon
of salt** and a **scant ½ teaspoon of baking soda.** Stir in.

Add **½ cup of rye flour** and stir in.

Kneading

Pour **1 cup of white flour** onto your kneading board and dump the batter onto it.

Knead in.

This dough never stops being sticky, so you can expect to use about another ½ **cup of white flour** to sprinkle the board as you knead. We want a dough that can just be handled. (You may even have to flour your hands to shape the loaves.)

Once you have that cup of white flour kneaded in, however, the bread requires only about another easy 5 minutes of kneading.

During this last 5 minutes, knead in **1 tablespoon of caraway seeds**—enough to let the eater know there is caraway in the bread without making it a "caraway bread."

(If you want caraway in only one or two of the loaves, divide the dough—after the required 5 minutes of kneading—into three parts, and knead a teaspoon of caraway seeds into each loaf that you want seeded. Knead just enough to disperse the seeds.)

Grease two baking sheets. (The loaves rise and spread too much to fit all three of them on one sheet.)

Sprinkle some **white cornmeal** over the sheets and shake to spread evenly. (I use white cornmeal instead of yellow because the New York bakeries I know use white cornmeal for their pumpernickels—perhaps for the contrast.)

Shaping the Loaves

Divide the dough into thirds and shape the three pieces into three loaves. I recommend oblong rather than round loaves—they rise a bit better and make better sandwiches.

Lay the loaves on the greased and cornmealed baking sheets, well apart.

With a sharp knife slash each loaf diagonally with three slashes, ¼–½ inch deep. (You don't have to worry about making the loaves fall as you did when slashing French Bread—there hasn't been any rise yet.)

Rising

Cover the loaves with a clean towel, and put into a warm, draft-free place to rise for 2–3 hours.

When the loaves are well-risen—and they will look

well-risen, with the slashes gaping wide—slash again, right into the same slashes. Only this time be careful: slash gently so as to avoid making the loaves fall.

Now, as with the French Breads, spray or brush the loaves with water. We want to make certain the crust is good and thick.

Spray again after the bread has been in the oven for about 10 minutes.

Baking

Bake in a moderate oven (about 350°–375°) for about 40 minutes, then, when and if the bread tests *almost* done, shut the oven off and allow it to stay in the closed oven for another 10 minutes. This is to prevent the scorching that Pumpernickels are prone to.

By the way—after about 25 minutes, you might want to reverse the top and bottom trays to prevent scorching.

After the loaves have been baking for 30 minutes, remove them from the oven and glaze with an **egg yolk** diluted with a tablespoon of water, brushed on with a pastry brush or your fingers. As soon as you've put the glaze on a loaf, sprinkle it with **caraway seeds,** if desired.

Return to the oven and finish baking.

Cool on a wire rack and serve hot.

Be sure to let your family see you take these loaves out of the oven—it's the only way you'll convince them they didn't come from the bakery.

SOUR PUMPERNICKEL—SUMMARY

A. 1 cup starter
   2 cups reconstituted skim milk
   2 tbsp. blackstrap molasses
   ¼ cup vegetable oil
   1 cup white flour
   1 cup rye flour
   2 cups whole wheat flour

B. 1 tbsp. sea salt
   ½ scant tsp. baking soda

C. ½ cup rye flour

D. 1–1½ cups white flour

E. 1 tbsp. caraway seeds

The first day make up the sponge by combining A into a large bowl. Cover and put into a draft-free place to rise.

The second day stir down the sponge, sprinkle B over its surface, and work in.

Stir in C.

Spread most of D over kneading board and dump batter onto the board, adding flour to the board as necessary during the kneading.

Knead for 5 minutes or so, working in E.

Grease two baking sheets; then sprinkle them with **white cornmeal.**

Divide the dough into three parts, shape into loaves, lay on the sheets, and slash three or four times to a depth of almost a half inch.

Rise for 2–3 hours.

When risen, slash again, gently.

Spray with water before going into the oven and again after 10 minutes baking.

After 30 minutes of baking, glaze with an **egg-yolk-and-water glaze** (1 yolk to 1 tablespoon of water) and sprinkle with additional **caraway seeds.**

Bake at about 350°–375° for about 40 minutes, then test for doneness. If almost done, shut off the oven and leave the loaves in for another 10 minutes.

Cool on a wire rack.

SOUR RYE

Here is a traditional bread, adapted for a bit more nutritive value without losing a bit of its delicious flavor or good looks.

"Sour Rye" is what it says when you buy the packaged bread in a market, or it may be known as Jewish Rye, or even New York Rye, but it's all the same bread.

You'll notice that the recipe calls for 2 cups of milk—or any liquid. That's quite literal. You could use plain water or fruit juice or chicken soup or beer. The liquid used makes only a small difference to the final flavor (but then, the difference between something good and something special is only a small difference). I like to use soup stock.

Rye flour tends to make for a heavyish bread, so you don't want to force in more of the white flour than the minimum required to handle the dough. I remind you that whole grain doughs tend to feel wetter inside than all-white doughs. So, don't strive for a dry dough; let the dough be as moist as it can be, just this side of too sticky.

This bread is kneaded more than the Sour Pumpernickel (a very close cousin) because the proportion of rye flour is higher. Remember, rye flour has almost no gluten, and so you must work the wheat flour until its gluten is developed enough to carry both itself and the rye—an ideal situation which in reality you never quite achieve.

A reason that some bought rye breads seem quite light and fluffy compared to home baked (apart from being machine-kneaded and aerated that way) is that some commercial bakers use very little rye flour and substitute caramel or some other coloring matter to get the look of rye—a solution that doesn't have my sympathy.

SOUR RYE

The First Day:
 1 cup starter
 2 cups milk—or any liquid
 ¼ cup vegetable oil
 2 tbsp. blackstrap molasses
 2 cups whole rye flour
 2 cups unbleached white flour
The Second Day:
 1 tbsp. sea salt
 ½ scant tsp. baking soda
 1 cup whole rye flour
 2–2½ cups unbleached white flour (enough white to knead)
For Greasing:
 melted butter or margarine, white cornmeal for sprinkling
Equipment:
 mixing bowl and spoon, kneading board, baking sheets

The First Day

In a large mixing bowl, stir together **1 cup of starter, 2 cups of milk** (or any liquid), **¼ cup of oil, 2 tablespoons of blackstrap molasses, 2 cups of rye flour,** and **2 cups of white flour,** until all is smooth.

Cover with a wet towel, and put into a draft-free place to rise overnight (or 12 hours).

The Second Day

Stir down the risen sponge.

Sprinkle over the surface of the stirred-down sponge **1 tablespoon of salt** and a **scant ½ teaspoon of baking soda,** and stir in.

Add the remaining **rye flour (1 cup)** to the mixture in the bowl and work in, wetting all the flour.

Kneading

Pour **1 cup of white flour** onto your kneading board and dump the batter onto it. Until you've worked in this cup, the dough will seem very loose.

Add another **cup of white flour,** and knead it in.

When you've kneaded in enough flour, sprinkle on your board only enough additional flour to keep this normally sticky dough manageable.

Knead for about 10 minutes, until the dough feels springy—resistant to your push—or until you can see the wrinkles on its surface.

When your dough is ready, grease two baking sheets and sprinkle them with **white cornmeal.**

Shaping the Loaves

Divide the dough into three equal parts and shape the loaves until the top surfaces look smooth, then place on the sheets.

Slash diagonally with a sharp knife about a half inch deep (three or four slashes per loaf), cover with a clean towel, and put in a warm place to rise for 2–3 hours. The slashes will gape wide open when the bread is ready.

Baking

Bake for 40 minutes at about 350°–375°, and then, if it tests almost done, in the oven with flame off for another 10 minutes.

Cool on a wire rack.

For best slicing, wait until the bread is fairly cool.

Options

☞ If you want a thicker crust, **spray** the loaves with water before putting them in the oven, and then again after they've been in for 5 minutes.

☞ If you like the shininess of the bakery loaf (they achieve it by glazing with a cornstarch solution), you can **glaze** with a smearing of **thinned egg** (1 tablespoon of egg to 1 teaspoon of water) 10 minutes before you shut off the oven. (Then use the remaining egg for scrambled eggs.) Don't glaze too thickly or you'll get yellow streaks.

☞ When you apply the glaze you can sprinkle on some **caraway seeds.** The glaze stays wet for a moment or two—time enough to sprinkle the seeds.

☞ If you want to add **caraway seeds, dill seeds, Russian caraway,** or **sesame seeds** to the bread proper, use a tablespoon of seeds for the entire batch, kneaded in when you've added the flour; or a teaspoon per loaf, kneaded in when you shape the loaves.

SOUR RYE—SUMMARY

A. 1 cup starter
2 cups milk (or other liquid)
¼ cup oil
2 tbsp. blackstrap molasses
2 cups rye flour
2 cups white flour

B. 1 tbsp. sea salt
½ tsp. baking soda

C. 1 cup rye flour

D. 2–2½ cups white flour

The first day mix A into a large bowl, until smooth.
The second day stir down the sponge, and mix in B.
Add C and work in.
Pour 1 cup of D onto kneading board, dump batter onto board, and knead.
Knead in another cup of D—and as much more as required to keep the dough from sticking.
Knead for 10 minutes.
Shape into three loaves.
Grease two baking sheets and sprinkle with **white cornmeal.**
Lay loaves on sheets and slash to a depth of a half inch, diagonally, three or four slashes per loaf.

Cover and rise in a warm place for 2–3 hours.

Bake in a 350°–375° oven for 40 minutes, then for another 10 minutes with the flame off (if the bread tests almost done).

Allow to cool for best slices.

SNACK BREADS

If you're looking for a light, airily textured bread, with a delicate flavor—just perfect for watercress and cucumber sandwiches—*keep looking because this is not it.*

But, if you're looking for a chewy, strong-flavored sour bread that's great with cheese or salami or tongue or liverwurst or hors d'oeuvres—you've arrived!

I invented this bread for my husband's thirty-fifth birthday party, making it right to his order: sour-ryish but chewier, with plenty of seeds, in long thin loaves, just right for a buffet.

Snack Bread comes only in this small size because it's too heavy a bread for large sandwich loaves—though if you like a heavy sandwich, go ahead and try it.

This is a backward bread, really: instead of working for lightness and rise and good texture, as with almost every other bread, here we are looking for a solid toughness that would mark failure in any other recipe.

You can use various kinds of seeds in Snack Breads —caraway, dark caraway (also known as Russian caraway or *tchernetsa*), dill, poppy, celery—it's up to you. Our favorite is the burnt flavor of the dark caraway, and I use plenty. But you've got to please yourself, so adjust the seeds to your own taste.

Risen in a warm place for about half an hour, these loaves will show some expansion, but not much; so don't expect these to double in size before baking. This is a heavy bread—deliberately.

SNACK BREADS

>   Yesterday:
>   1 cup starter
>   1¾ cups hot water
>   2 tbsp. honey
>   4 cups whole wheat flour
>   Today:
>   2 tbsp. sea salt
>   2 tbsp. seeds (caraway or dark caraway or dill or fen-
>   nel, etc.)
>   1 cup whole rye flour or rye meal
>   For Greasing:
>   melted margarine or butter
>   Equipment:
>   mixing bowl and spoon, kneading board, baking sheets

First Day

The night before you plan to bake the bread, make up the
sponge: into a large mixing bowl measure **1 cup of sourdough starter** (whole wheat starter if you have it, but
white is fine), **1¾ cups of hot tap water,** and **2 tablespoons
of honey,** stirring it all to dissolve the honey.

Stir in **4 cups of whole wheat flour,** until your mixture is smooth.

Cover the bowl with wax paper or plastic wrap and
set it aside in a draft-free place overnight. (If you get the
inspiration early enough in the morning, you can make
these breads the same day, because this sponge needs
only 8 or 9 hours to work.)

Second Day

Uncover the sponge and stir it down.

Stir into the sponge **2 tablespoons of salt** and **2 tablespoons** of your favorite **seeds.** (More if, like my husband,
you're a real seed freak; less if your tastes run milder.)

Kneading

Spread a **cup of rye flour or rye meal** on the kneading
board, and dump the sponge onto it.

Knead in the rye flour (if more than a cup is needed

to make it stop sticking to the board, use additional
whole wheat—you don't want to use more than one cup
of rye). Remember, this is a whole grain bread; the finished dough is supposed to feel *moister* than the finished
dough of a white bread. So don't keep adding flour until
the dough feels dry.

This is one bread where skimping on the kneading
won't matter at all, so knead only a couple of minutes
more.

Shaping the Loaves

When you've finished kneading, divide the dough into
four pieces and roll out the loaves.

Flour the board lightly—just to keep it from sticking, not to add more flour—and, starting in the middle,
roll the dough into a single strand an inch thick. (That
should make it just long enough to fit onto a large baking
sheet—if your sheet is too short, cut off the excess and
make five shorter loaves.)

As each loaf is rolled out, lay it on a greased baking
sheet, two per sheet.

When the four loaves are rolled out, put the sheets
into a warm place, cover, and allow to rise for ½–¾ hour.

Baking

There will be little discernible rise in the loaves, but, if
there is none at all, allow to rise for another 15 minutes.

We don't slash this bread—so don't be shocked when
it cracks along the side.

Bake at about 350° for 30–40 minutes, and, when you
think they're done, test. Don't allow the small size of the
loaf to fool you into thinking that it *must* be done. There
is no *must* about it. Whole grain breads—especially rye
breads—can be stubborn that way, taking longer to bake
on a damp day, or just because you're in a hurry.

Cool on a wire rack, and when you come to slicing it,
slice it thin with a serrated knife: the crust is a tough
one and a plain knife could easily slip.

SNACK BREADS—SUMMARY

A. 1 cup starter
   1¾ cups hot water
   2 tbsp. honey
   4 cups whole wheat flour

B. 2 tbsp. sea salt
   2 tbsp. seeds

C. 1 cup rye flour or
   rye meal

The first day combine A in a large bowl until smooth. Cover and put in a draft-free place to rise overnight.

The second day stir down, then add B, mixing in thoroughly.

Spread C on your kneading board, dump sponge onto board, and knead in. (If more flour is required to flour board, use whole wheat.)

Knead for a few more minutes.

Grease two baking sheets.

Divide the dough into quarters and shape each quarter into a long, thin loaf—about 1 inch thick.

Lay the loaves on the greased sheets.

Rise for ½–¾ hour.

Bake 30–40 minutes at about 350°.

Test, then cool on a wire rack.

Cut with a serrated knife.

6

Spiral
Breads

Here's a bread that can keep your family interested day after day, because, like Cleopatra (a noted Egyptian bread baker), custom cannot stale its infinite variety.

It is called Spiral Bread because the dough is rolled out to a thickness of about one quarter inch, and then rolled up into the shape of a loaf. We spread the flattened dough with various fillings, so that when sliced the spiral is evident to the eye and the palate.

There is virtually no limit to the variations you can try with this bread. Different herb combinations give you a bread to complement (or contrast with) any main course; small bits of meat or shrimp give you a bread that's a main course in itself; various sweet combinations give you a dessert bread.

Don't be afraid to let the kids help you here. Their imaginations are particularly fertile in dreaming up combinations, and they will get a big kick out of helping to roll out the dough and sprinkling on the herbs. And don't worry about their using too much of an herb; there are very few herbs that can be "too much" in this bread. You'd be surprised how much of most herbs you need to really maintain the flavor after baking.

This is also a rich dough, though, without eggs, not quite as rich as the Rich Whole Wheat. But it's just as easy to handle—a necessity for this bread.

It is also a great dough for rolls. I'll describe Kaiser Rolls (Hard Rolls) and Knots after we've made the bread.

Before we get on to the baking let's talk about the fillings.

Herb Fillings

In class, I usually plan one herb filling, and then put out all my herbs and seeds for the class to invent a combination of their own. The planned filling is invariably grated Parmesan cheese (enough to cover the whole of the rolled-out dough with a thin layer), oregano, fennel seed, and basil. With this, as with all herb fillings, I butter the rolled-out dough with melted margarine or butter before scattering the cheese. This greasing helps the separate swirls of the spiral to stand out after baking.

As for the invented fillings, they are always different, and always interesting and tasty: minced onion or garlic; celery seed and celery salt and grated cheese; seasoned salt and thyme and tarragon; dill seed and dill weed and savory.

The list could go on and on. There is no herb you can't use, no combination you shouldn't try.

Main Course Fillings

This is not my favorite way to use these breads, so I don't emphasize them in class, but they are fine with bits of raw shrimp and fennel seed spread over the buttered surface, or with bits of chopped meat, or even with certain unnamable unhealthy things like sausage.

Just roll them up and bake like any other bread.

Sweet Fillings

Here's where the compliments get extravagant.

The recipe makes three loaves, and after the planned herb loaf and the invented herb loaf, my class makes the third loaf with cinnamon honey.

To make cinnamon honey, mix 4 teaspoons of cinnamon with 1 cup of honey (or maple syrup or maple sugar, if you have it). This is more than you will use for one loaf of bread (or even two loaves), but it can be kept in a covered jar for the next time you bake Cinnamon Spiral— and you will bake it again—or for cinnamon toast, or for spooning over hot cereals.

We don't butter this one. Just brush the cinnamon honey over the rolled-out dough.

Two of my students invented a delicious healthful alternative to this bread: Honey-Carob Spiral. For those of you who don't know carob, it is ground-up dried St. John's bread (a seed pod from a tree), and it is a healthful substitute for chocolate.

Take a brush and spread about 3 tablespoons of honey over the rolled-out dough and then sprinkle about 3 tablespoons of carob powder over the honey. Add nuts if you like.

I don't recommend jam because it is made with white sugar, but one of my students swears by a thin jam filling.

Make up your own combinations.

SPIRAL BREAD

For the Dough:
2 tbsp. active dry yeast
2 tsp. sea salt
2 tbsp. honey
2 cups hot water
½ cup skim milk powder
¼ cup vegetable oil
1 cup raw wheat germ
5–6 cups unbleached white flour

For the Filling:
(whatever you like)

For Greasing:
melted butter or margarine

Equipment:
large mixing bowl, spoon or whisk, kneading board, rolling pin, optional pastry brush, 3 baking pans

Mixing

Into a large mixing bowl measure and combine **2 tablespoons of yeast, 2 teaspoons of salt, 2 tablespoons of honey,** and **2 cups of hot tap water.** Stir.

Mix in **½ cup of skim milk powder** (¼ cup if noninstant).

Stir in **¼ cup of vegetable oil.**

Mix in **1 cup of raw wheat germ** and the first **4 cups of flour,** 2 cups at a time.

Kneading

Spread a **fifth cup** over the kneading board and scrape the batter out onto the flour. Knead in. The dough will be very wet.

A little bit at a time, add as much of the remaining cup (#6) as required to make the dough stop sticking.

After that, use only light sprinklings during kneading: this dough should be light.

Knead for a brisk 5 minutes (or a lazy, easy 10 minutes).

First Rise

When fully kneaded (at which point the wrinkles should show beautifully on this bread), drip a few drops of oil (or melted butter or margarine) in the scraped-out bowl; drop in the dough ball; turn over a few times to oil all sides; cover with a clean, dry towel; and put in a very warm, draft-free place to rise.

This dough is likely to rise somewhat faster than most; if the day is warm, the rise can be finished in 45 minutes. But don't go by the clock: finger-test (see p. 54).

If your fingerprint stays in the dough, punch down, and knead gently for a minute to get rid of the larger bubbles.

Rolling Out

Divide the dough into three equal pieces.

At this point, when baking for myself, I put one third in a bowl and stick it in the fridge for a later bread or for Pizza (ah! the magic in that word—I only have to write the word "Pizza" and my husband comes into the room), set another third aside for Rolls, and make the third into a Spiral Bread. But you know your appetite.

I'll describe the making of one Spiral loaf, and you can repeat it for as many loaves as you wish.

Sprinkle a thin layer of flour onto your board. You may have to make a few such sprinklings through the course of the rolling. Put the ball of dough on the floured board and begin to flatten it out by pressing it with your hand or pushing it with your fingers. Turn the dough over and repeat.

You'll want to turn the dough over several times in the course of this flattening—it helps keep it from sticking. If you do all your patting and rolling on one side, I guarantee that the dough will stick and pull apart when you try to roll it up.

If the dough shows any sign of sticking when you turn it, give it a little sprinkling of flour.

As you poke and flatten try to keep the shape of the dough roughly rectangular.

Now, take your rolling pin and roll the dough out to a rectangular shape, a quarter of an inch thick. Watch out for the edges; they tend to want to be thicker. Continue to turn the dough over between rollings. Keep the shape rectangular.

If, despite your best efforts, the shape insists on having some nonrectangular portions, cut them off and throw them onto another piece of dough. (Should you need to cut and patch, water applied with your fingertips becomes the glue to hold the sections of dough together.)

When you achieve the $\frac{1}{4}$-inch thickness, turn the dough over, and put on your fillings (see pp. 117–119), right out to the edges. Be generous: this is a loaf of bread, not a piece of toast. (With sweet fillings, however, it's better not to be too generous: they come out very sweet.)

Rolling Up

We now have a slab of dough about $\frac{1}{4}$ inch thick, and spread with a combination to suit our taste. So, take a deep breath and relax.

The way you roll this loaf depends on the pan you want to put it in. Sometimes, my students like to put a Spiral Bread into a ring mold. In that case, we start rolling from the long side of the rectangle of dough, to get as long a loaf as we can. Sometimes the loaf goes into a regular loaf pan, in which case we start rolling from the short side of the rectangle, for as short a loaf as we can get. Spiral Breads can even be done free-standing on a baking sheet—in which case, roll it any way you please.

The secret of a successful Spiral is to roll tightly, making sure there are no air spaces as you roll. Roll slowly and evenly, not letting any part get too far ahead, checking often for air pockets, pushing the dough along with the flats of your fingers. (As you roll, you may have to pull out the edges of the dough to keep the rectangle.)

If the dough insists on sticking to the board a little, don't worry and don't force it. Take a scraper or a knife and gently loosen the dough. If, as instructed, you've turned the dough over during the rolling-out, the sticking won't be serious.

When you've rolled the entire filled rectangle (it's

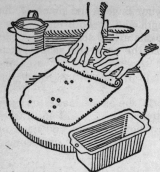

Rolling from the short
side to fit a loaf pan

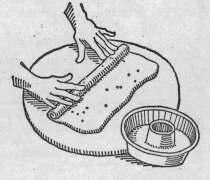

Rolling from the long
side to fit a ring mold

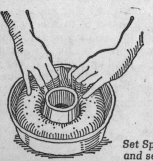

Set Spiral in ring mold
and seal the ends together.

easier than it sounds), wet your fingers and pinch all the
seams closed, along the length and at both ends. Sweet
fillings will run out if the seams aren't sealed. For a ring
mold don't seal the ends; join the ends and seal them to
each other.

Now, grease your pan and put the loaf in, seam side
down. If the loaf is too short for the pan, don't be afraid
to give it a gentle pull to make it longer. If it's too long,
don't be afraid to push it together. Procrustean as it
seems, you can do all this without losing the spiral.

Rising the Loaf

If you are doing a Cinnamon Spiral, spray the top with
a little water and dribble over a bit more cinnamon. For
Honey-Carob Spiral, spray and top with more carob
powder.

For Cheese-Herb Spiral, butter the outside of the
loaf (or smear it with egg white) and, if you like, sprinkle
on additional cheese.

Cover with a clean, dry towel and put in a warm,
draft-free place to rise for about half an hour.

The loaf will by no means double, but it will swell
appreciably. (If you're rushed, this rise can be skimped
a little.)

Baking

When risen, bake in a 350°–360° oven for 30–40 minutes.
Test with a clean knife for doneness (see pp. 21–23).
There is a problem with testing the sweet Spirals.
Whether your filling is cinnamon and honey, honey and
carob, jam, or some other sweet, the melting of the sweet
can give a knife test that seems to indicate rawness.

You have to inspect your knife quite carefully; is
that streaking really raw dough, or is it simply wet honey
and carob?

Sometimes, the only way to tell is by cutting a loaf
in half.

Try to serve this one hot.

A warning: Make certain your dough is rolled out to
¼-inch thickness, and that you roll it up tight. If your

dough is thick and/or your roll too loose, the bread will come apart in the baking, and form internal arches—good for catacombs, but disappointing in bread.

Options

☞ If you are making all herb breads from this recipe you may want to add some **herbs** right into the dough. If so, put them in the mixing bowl after you add the hot water.

☞ You can double the **milk powder** to a full cup. No further adjustments will be required. Or make the bread with **whole milk**. If Spirals are your children's favorite, use super-milk—that is, whole milk plus milk powder. If you don't warm the whole milk, triple the rising time.

☞ If you wish, you may omit the buttering of the Herb Spirals—the difference is a subtle one.

KAISER ROLLS AND KNOT ROLLS

These two rolls have no real relationship to Spiral Breads: they are included here because this dough is particularly good for making rolls. Kaiser and Knot Rolls can be made from any kneaded dough. There's nothing to stop you from using, say, the Rich Whole Wheat dough and making yourself a brown Kaiser.

Kaiser Rolls

Kaiser Rolls are made very much like a pinwheel.

The entire recipe makes about 24 rolls. Or you can make 8 rolls with a third of the dough and refrigerate the rest.

Pinch off handball-sized bits of dough (or divide your third of the batter into eight parts), roll them into balls, then flatten them into rounds 4 to 4½ inches across. (You may have to flour your board lightly.)

Take one edge of the circle, lift it, and bring it into the center of the round. With your finger, press down the right side of the triangle you've just made.

Press firmly along the
inside of the flap.

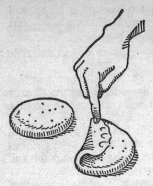

Lift the point . . .

And press it into the center.

Continue around, clockwise,
pressing only the right side
of each flap.

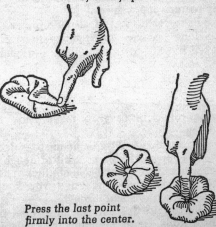

Press the last point
firmly into the center.

Move to the right, and lift the point which you've just created by pressing that seam and bring this point into the center, slightly overlapping the first fold.

Once again, with your finger, press down the right edge.

And again, moving to the right, lift the point end of the seam, and slightly overlap the points you've already made, and press down on the right side of the dough with your fingers.

The process is performed six times in all; the sixth time you don't press down the side of the triangle, but you do press firmly in the center, to make certain the roll doesn't open in the baking.

Set the rolls to rise for about half an hour, covered with a clean towel.

Put a couple of cups of water up to boil, because we're going to treat these rolls as if they were French Bread, so as to get a nice, crisp, crackling crust.

When risen, spray the rolls with water.

Put a shallow container into the bottom of the oven and pour in the boiling water.

Put your rolls in the oven and set it at 350°.

After 5 minutes, spray again.

After 15 minutes, take them from the oven, brush with **egg white,** and sprinkle on your favorite seeds. (I prefer **Russian caraway seeds,** but the delicatessens usually feature **poppy seeds.**)

Bake for a total of 25–30 minutes. (These rolls take this long because you remove them from the oven to glaze. If you omit sprayings and glazing, 20 minutes will do.)

Knot Rolls

These rolls are easy to make and very professional-looking.

The recipe will make about four dozen small rolls.

In your hands, shape a bit of dough until it's about 8 inches long and about $\frac{1}{2}$–$\frac{3}{4}$ inch thick. Then twist this rope into a simple overhand knot. You know, make a little loop and pass one end through.

Put to rise for half an hour, then treat just like the Kaiser Rolls. Or forget about the seeds, if you prefer.

Knot Rolls

SPIRAL BREADS—SUMMARY

A. 2 tbsp. active dry
   yeast
   2 tsp. sea salt
   2 tbsp. honey
   2 cups hot water

B. ½ cup skim milk powder

C. ¼ cup vegetable oil

D. 1 cup raw wheat germ

E. 5–6 cups flour

Combine A into a large mixing bowl and stir.

Dissolve in B.

Stir in C.

Mix in D and the first 4 cups of E, 2 cups at a time.

Spread another cup of E over kneading board. Scrape batter onto board and knead in. (Add more until dough stops sticking, then sprinkle as needed.)

Knead briskly for 5 minutes.

Rise.

Finger-test and then punch down.

Pat and roll out dough into a rectangle, turning frequently and flouring board as required, until dough is ¼ inch thick.

Spread desired filling over dough.

Roll up tightly and evenly.

Seal seams with wet fingers.

Grease appropriate pan and put loaf in it. Cover and put to rise.

Wet top of loaf lightly and sprinkle on more of filling.

When risen, bake at around 360° for 30–40 minutes.

Test with a clean knife. Serve hot.

7

Rye
Breads
and
Pumpernickel

Rye is a low gluten (but not a nongluten) flour, which means that in an all-rye bread you would have to work like blue blazes to develop elasticity enough to hold some rise—and would still wind up with a bread two inches high.

Then why bother with Rye Bread at all? Well, if you ask that question, you've never tasted Rye Bread. I don't mean the kind of 1-cup-of-rye-to-3-cups-of-white bread that you'll find in most bakeries; that only gives you the barest hint of the great taste. Rye Breads are in a class by themselves when it comes to flavor (a class rivaled but not surpassed by Sourdough Breads).

Rye Breads are traditionally Northern European breads —German, Scandinavian, Russian. There is some difference between the breads made in Europe and the breads made here. Different strains of rye and wheat grow here. (Even the same strains take on somewhat different characteristics when grown in different soil.)

Russian peasants make a "black" bread from very dark flour, coarsely ground. But there is no equivalent flour in this country—and probably not in Russia today —so, to get a "black" bread I use blackstrap molasses: the federal government permits commercial bakers to use a whole string of chemical colorings.

While the four breads that make up this chapter aren't by any stretch of the imagination black, they are dark, and our Pumpernickel is *quite* dark. They are all delicious, with a delightful aroma, but by no means easy to make: in fact, two of them are out-and-out hard.

Rye flour is harder to handle than wheat. It looks

different and it feels different. It's stickier, which makes for more difficult kneading—yet it must be kneaded longer. Rye doughs are more moist, which means that to have a light-textured bread we never get the dough as dry as we do with wheat flour. (Do you remember what we did with Italian Bread to get a better web? Flattening the dough out and rolling it up? Well, don't try that here— rye dough will stick to the board!)

Of the four Rye Breads presented here, Potato Rye is the hardest to make up because it has the most rye flour; Refrigerator Rye is the easiest because it uses half white flour.

Pumpernickel is harder to make up than Refrigerator Rye, but easier than Swedish or Potato Rye. (Pumpernickel gives a higher and lighter loaf than the latter breads, with all the chewiness and flavor that makes it such a favorite in my classes.)

All the breads in this chapter require a great deal of kneading. Even after all the flour is in, you'll want to knead for another 15 minutes or more to develop as much of the gluten as you can.

If you've never made a kneaded bread before and want to try a rye bread first, start with Refrigerator Rye (but read pp. 129–130). It bears the closest resemblance to a "normal" bread, kneading up more quickly, with no worry about when the first rise is finished.

There are other problems with Rye Breads. For one, with Potato Rye and Swedish Rye you can't depend on the finger test to tell you when the dough is sufficiently risen. The dough of these two breads develops a minimum of gluten, and will hold a fingerprint *as soon as you finish kneading*, because of the low level of elasticity. So, for these two breads, don't use the finger test. Assume a rise (in a warm place, of course) of 1½–2 hours, and keep looking at the dough. Much as I hate to resort to that old catch phrase, the dough has risen enough when it has "doubled in bulk," which means that it will take up about twice as much room in the rising bowl. Be sure you take a good look when you put the dough to rise—remember its size and level in the bowl.

With Refrigerator Rye and Pumpernickel you can use the finger test.

There is another problem with Rye Breads. Rye

dough tends to "draw wet," which means that the bread
can be baked enough to be fit for eating, and still show
streaks when you test it with a knife for doneness. (Refrigerator Rye isn't as much a problem this way as the
others.) Use the knife test by all means. It will still show
you whether or not you have gobs of unbaked dough. But
if the knife draws out a few *streaks* (not dough), tap the
loaf on the bottom. A done loaf will give quite a hollow
tom-tom sound.

I know this sounds inexact—but so much of baking
is.

Remember—you can always cut a loaf open to see
if it's done. If it's not, you can put it back in the oven.
The cut will not heal, but the bread will finish baking.

Share the making of these breads with a friend—
someone to relieve you and take over part of the kneading; I never make a Rye Bread without my husband.

If you don't have someone to help, knead in spurts,
covering the dough with the mixing bowl while you rest.
The dough doesn't care if it's kneaded in five 3-minute
chunks, or in one 15-minute sprint.

More than other breads, Ryes like an occasional
flouring of the kneading board—even after "enough"
flour is in.

Also, you'll have to clean your hands off more often;
as I said, rye is stickier. Spill a little flour between your
palms and rub away as much dough (onto the dough
ball) as you can. Then take a spoon or a scraper and
scrape away what remains. (You'll see what I mean
within the first minute of kneading Potato or Swedish
Rye.)

Are you discouraged? Don't be. These are rewarding
breads, healthful and great-tasting—and like nothing
you'll find in a bakery.

POTATO RYE

Potato Rye, and Swedish Rye which follows, should be
rated "X"—for adults only; the flavors are too definite
for kids.

Potato Rye is an old, traditional recipe, with European—especially German—roots, combining two peasant standbys, flour and potatoes.

This is quite different from any other bread in the book. It has no sweetener, neither honey nor molasses. The mashed potatoes and potato water are what feed the yeast. Of course, the flour will feed the yeast, too, but that is a slower process, while the carbohydrates in the potato are quickly converted, although not as quickly as honey or molasses.

Because it is such a great yeast-feeder, this water that the potatoes have cooked in should never be thrown away: it is an excellent bread-baking liquid.

The potato also helps to solidify the texture, making for a satisfying, crusty, heavy, solid bread—though by no means too heavy.

Both the mashed potato and the potato water should be hot when they are used, as hot as the hot tap water which we've used in most other recipes, so unless you have just cooked up the potatoes, heat them. If you use them cold, you'll slow down the rising time by hours. But, when you heat them, don't allow the water to boil. One of the few times I ever killed yeast was with this bread—bringing the potato water (with the potatoes in it) to a boil, and then not waiting for it to cool before throwing in the yeast. To avoid this, stick your finger in the water before you add it to the yeast. If you can hold your finger in it for a few seconds (no heroics, please), fine. If it feels too hot, wait a while or cool it down with a little cold potato water. Better to be safe than have dead yeast.

This bread is not a high riser. It is certainly higher than all-rye breads, but not nearly as high as the other loaves we've been working with.

But that's the nature of rye, and it still makes good toast and great eating.

POTATO RYE

For the Dough:
  2 tbsp. active dry yeast
  1 tbsp. sea salt
  1 tbsp. caraway seeds
  2 cups hot potato water
  1 packed cup hot mashed potatoes
  4 cups whole rye flour
  2–2½ cups whole wheat flour
For Greasing:
  melted butter or margarine
  cornmeal
Equipment:
  large mixing bowl, mixing spoon, kneading board,
  large baking sheet

Mixing

Into a large mixing bowl, measure **2 tablespoons of yeast,
1 tablespoon of salt, 1 tablespoon of caraway seeds,** and
2 cups of hot (but not boiling or near-boiling) **potato
water,** and stir.

Add **1 cup of hot mashed potatoes.** Mix until the
mashed potato has been distributed fairly evenly throughout.

Stir in the **4 cups of rye flour,** 2 cups at a time. (The
mixture will appear grayish—don't worry.)

Add **1 cup of whole wheat flour** to the bowl and
mix in.

Kneading

Spread **1 cup of whole wheat flour** over your kneading
board, scrape the batter onto the flour, and knead it. There
will be very little resistance or cohesion until you have
the whole cup well in.

Continue to knead for 15 minutes, adding as much of
an additional ½ **cup of whole wheat flour** to the board as
necessary to handle the dough.

Remember, this dough never really gets dry. On the
surface (if you don't dig your fingers into it), it will be
rather less sticky, but it should never really dry, staying
even wetter than the Whole Wheat Breads we've done.

If, after 15 minutes, you are not feeling resistance

when you knead, knead for another 5 or 10 minutes. It is very important to develop all the gluten you can.

First Rise

When the dough shows signs of good resistance as you knead, stop, scrape the dough off your hands, drip a few drops of oil into the scraped-out but unwashed bowl, drop the dough in, oil all sides, and put to rise in a very warm, draft-free place, covered with a hot, wet towel. (Like whole wheat dough, the rye will crust if the towel isn't wet and warm.)

You'll want it to rise for about 1½–2 hours, or until the dough has about doubled in volume. (Don't skimp on this rising time.)

Remember, the finger test doesn't work for this bread.

Shaping The Loaves

When doubled, punch down and knead out any large air bubbles, right in the bowl.

Dump the dough ball onto your kneading board, and cut in half.

Knead each half into a smooth ball, then shape into a loaf, about 8 by 4 inches, and as high as you can make it.

Grease a baking sheet large enough to hold your two good-sized loaves (they will swell), and sprinkle with **cornmeal** (for a good bottom crust).

Lay the loaves on the sheets, spaced well apart, and, with a sharp or serrated knife, slash each loaf with three or four diagonal slashes to a depth of about one-half inch.

Rising the Loaves

Cover with a clean, *dry* towel (a moist towel would stick to the loaves, causing them to fall when you removed it), and put back in that very warm, draft-free place to rise for 30 minutes to an hour (about half the time of the first rise).

The slashes will gape wide when the bread is well risen, and the loaves will look considerably larger. If you aren't certain the loaves have risen enough, wait a bit more.

When risen, remove the towel and spray, brush, or sprinkle the loaves with water, to help get that marvelous, crunchy crust. Spray again after 15 minutes of baking.

Baking

Bake the loaves in a moderate oven (350°–375°) for 50 minutes, then leave in the hot oven *with the flame off* for another 10 minutes. After a knife test has shown you there are no large clumps of dough, thump the bottom crust for hollowness.

Here's something I've found helpful: if the bottoms are showing signs of getting burnt before the baking time is up, and the knife test shows signs of raw dough—turn the loaves over and let them bake for a few minutes *topside down.*

When done, remove from the oven, allow to cool on a wire rack for a half hour, and eat warm.

Options

☞ In all Rye Bread recipes, the substitution of all or part **rye meal** for the rye flour will give you a pleasant chewiness.

☞ If you want to include **wheat germ** or **bran** in this recipe (or the following recipes), substitute for the rye flour, not the whole wheat. We need all the gluten we can get.

☞ You could make the recipe easier to work (and less nutritious) by substituting **unbleached white flour** for all or part of the whole wheat. If you do, be sure to substitute ½ cup of wheat germ for an equal amount of rye.

☞ The kind and amount of **seeds** are very much a matter of taste. My husband, for example, thinks that 1 tablespoon of caraway seeds isn't enough by half. You may want to try **dark caraway seeds** for this bread, or **fennel seed** (as in the Swedish Rye that follows).

☞ After the spraying you could sprinkle a teaspoonful of **seeds** over the surface of each loaf.

POTATO RYE—SUMMARY

A. 2 tbsp. active dry yeast
1 tbsp. sea salt
1 tbsp. caraway seeds
2 cups hot potato water

B. 1 cup hot mashed potatoes

C. 4 cups whole rye flour

D. 2–2½ cups whole wheat flour

Combine A into a large mixing bowl and stir.

Add B and mix in.

Add C, 2 cups at a time. Stir in.

Mix in 1 cup of D.

Spread another cup of D over kneading board, scrape batter onto board, and knead in.

Add as much of remaining ½ cup as required to permit kneading, then knead for 15 minutes more.

Oil the dough in the mixing bowl, cover with a wet, hot, clean towel, and set to rise until doubled: about 1½–2 hours. Do not finger-test.

Punch down, knead out bubbles, then dump dough ball onto board and divide in half.

Shape two loaves, approximately 8 by 4 inches.

Grease a large baking sheet, sprinkle with cornmeal, and lay the loaves on the sheet, well apart.

Slash each loaf three or four times, a half inch deep.

Cover with a clean, dry towel, and replace in a warm, draft-free location for 30 minutes to an hour. (Look for the gaping of the slashes and for the increase in loaf size.)

When risen, spray with water. (Spray again after 15 minutes baking.)

Bake about 50 minutes at 350°–375°, then 10 minutes with flame off.

Thump the bottom for doneness. If done, the loaf should sound very hollow.

Cool on a wire rack for a half hour.

SWEDISH RYE

This is definitely the tastiest rye in the book, but really too savory for breakfast.

This is a traditional Swedish recipe (but made with

blackstrap molasses instead of corn syrup because I can't bring myself to use sugar syrups when molasses is so much better for me), and quite different from most of the kneaded breads we've made together.

Instead of slashing, we'll repeatedly prick the surface of the molded loaf with a fork.

Instead of working for a crisp crust, we'll try for a soft one, brushing the loaf tops with milk toward that end.

Instead of the standard loaf shape for whole grain breads, we'll shape these loaves like the French Bread baguettes.

When you shape the loaves, give a good bit of kneading to the individual thirds and shape them into smooth balls before you roll the dough out to long loaves. If there are folds in the dough, they won't disappear, and the bread might open along such a seam.

Although potato water is the liquid called for in this recipe, you have a wide range of liquids to choose from: skim milk or buttermilk are very Scandinavian; and beer is a popular liquid with Rye Breads. (See Options for amounts.) Whatever liquid you use, make certain it is hot (but not boiling). If you do not use potato water, increase the salt by 1 teaspoon.

This bread is slightly easier to work up than the Potato Rye. For one thing, there is a higher proportion of wheat flour in the recipe. For another, we use a ¼ cup of oil. That doesn't sound like much, but it does make a difference in ease of handling. But that doesn't mean you can skimp on the kneading. Don't.

The recipe tells you to mash the fennel seed in the mixing bowl with the back of a spoon, assuming that you don't own a mortar and pestle. If you do, by all means crush your fennel there and pour it into the bowl.

By the way, don't—unless you're desperate—use ground fennel. (If you do, use 1½ tablespoons.)

SWEDISH RYE

For the Dough:
    2 tbsp. fennel seed
    2 tbsp. active dry yeast
    ¼ cup blackstrap molasses
    ¼ cup honey
    2 cups hot potato water
    2 tsp. sea salt
    grated peel of 1 orange
    ¼ cup vegetable oil
    3 cups whole rye flour
    3½–4 cups whole wheat flour
For Greasing:
    melted margarine or butter
    cornmeal
For Crust:
    milk
Equipment:
    large mixing bowl, spoon or whisk, kneading board, 2
    baking sheets, pastry brush (optional)

Mixing

Drop **2 tablespoons of fennel seed** into your mixing bowl,
and crush it with the back of the bowl of a spoon. It's not
necessary to grind it up fine—just break the seeds open to
release the flavor.

Add **2 tablespoons of yeast, ¼ cup of blackstrap molasses** plus **¼ cup of honey** (measured into the same cup),
and **2 cups of hot potato water** (not boiling). Stir, to mix.

Add **2 tablespoons of salt,** the **grated peel** (just the
zest, the outer peel) **of 1 orange,** and **¼ cup of vegetable
oil.** Stir.

Mix in well, **3 cups of rye flour.**

Mix in **3 cups of whole wheat flour.**

Kneading

Spread **½ cup of whole wheat** over the kneading board and
scrape the batter onto the flour. Knead in.

Continue to knead for 15 minutes, using as much of
the remaining **½ cup of flour** as necessary for kneading.
Try not to go beyond 7 cups altogether.

First Rise

When well kneaded, drip a few drops of oil into the
scraped-out bowl; drop in the dough ball, oiling all surfaces; cover with a hot, wet, clean towel; and set in a very
warm, draft-free place to rise for about 1½ hours.

Again, the finger test won't tell us when the dough is
risen, so look for it to double in volume.

Shaping the Loaves

When risen, punch down, and knead in the bowl for a
minute to get rid of those big air bubbles.

Turn the dough onto the board and cut into three
pieces. Roll the dough into three smooth balls. Roll the
balls out into three loaves, about 2 by 14 inches. I know
these look quite thin, but they will swell—though never
as much as French Bread loaves.

Grease two baking sheets with melted butter or margarine, and sprinkle with a thin layer of **cornmeal.**

Lay the loaves out, two on one sheet, one on another.
Prick all over the top surface with a fork. (This gives quite
a different look to the loaf than slashing.)

Rising the Loaves

Cover with a clean, dry towel, and set in a very warm,
draft-free place to rise for 30–45 minutes. The loaves
should look considerably risen before you bake them.

When risen, brush the tops with a bit of milk (skim or
whole—it doesn't matter), using either a pastry brush
or your fingers. Whichever you use, be careful—these
loaves are very easy to knock down. (If you used beer as
your liquid, don't brush with milk, brush with beer.)

Baking

Bake in a 350°–375° oven for about 30 minutes.

Try using the knife test—sometimes it works for this
bread. At any rate—tap the bottom for the hollow sound.

Cool on a wire rack for a few minutes and serve hot.
The taste of the fennel seed and orange is mind-blowing.

Options

☞ If you want to use **beer** for your liquid, be sure it's warm (and increase the salt by 1 teaspoon). Use either 2 cups of beer, or 1 cup of beer and 1 cup of another liquid. Don't worry about curdling the **milk** or **buttermilk.** Bread doesn't care. Any **vegetable water** will do excellently in this bread (or in any bread, for that matter).

☞ Reducing or cutting out the **honey** will lower the calories. It will also reduce the keeping power of your bread.

☞ **Anise seed** is another traditional Scandinavian herb, so feel free to substitute anise for the fennel seed. But crush it, and don't use the ground stuff—it has no texture.

☞ If you prefer a **hard crust** to the soft one that is characteristic of this bread, spray twice with water (as with the Potato Rye) instead of using milk.

☞ **Rye meal** substituted for rye flour makes for a nice chewiness.

☞ As with Potato Rye, if you are substituting **wheat germ** or **bran,** do so for part of the rye flour.

SWEDISH RYE—SUMMARY

A. 2 tbsp. fennel seed

B. 2 tbsp. active dry
   yeast
   ¼ cup blackstrap
   molasses
   ¼ cup honey
   2 cups hot potato water

C. 2 tsp. sea salt
   grated peel of 1
   orange
   ¼ cup vegetable oil

D. 3 cups whole rye
   flour

E. 3½–4 cups whole
   wheat flour

   milk

With the back of a spoon, crush A in your mixing bowl.
   Add B and stir.
   Mix in C.
   Add D and mix in.
   Stir in 3 cups of E.
   Spread another ½ cup of E over the board and scrape batter onto board. Knead in.

Knead for 15 minutes, adding as much of remaining flour as necessary for kneading.

Oil the dough ball in the bowl; cover with a hot, wet, clean towel; rise in a warm place for about 1½ hours. Do not finger-test.

When risen, punch down, and knead for a few minutes in the bowl.

Dump onto kneading board and divide into three.

Roll each third into a smooth ball, then roll out into three long loaves, about 2 by 14 inches.

Lay loaves on greased and cornmealed baking sheets.

Prick all over top surfaces with a fork.

Cover with a clean, dry towel and rise for 30–45 minutes.

When risen, brush surface of loaves with milk.

Bake 350°–375° for about 30 minutes.

Thump the bottom for the hollow sound indicating doneness.

Cool on a wire rack, serve hot.

REFRIGERATOR RYE

If Potato Rye and Swedish Rye are rated "X," there's no doubt that Refrigerator Rye is rated "G." This bread is mild flavored—for a Rye—and made in loaf pans for a sandwich shape.

If this is your first experience with a Refrigerator Rise Bread, you might want to refer back to Chapter 3, where a couple of them are discussed.

This is the easiest of the Rye Breads we'll do. The gluten in the white flour makes it quicker to work up cohesion, and gives it a higher rise than the other rye doughs. Also, it requires less kneading, with less dough sticking to your hands, and less need to flour the board.

All in all, a good, simple Rye Bread without particular problems to watch for.

REFRIGERATOR RYE

For the Dough:
   2 tbsp. active dry yeast
   1 tbsp. sea salt
   ⅓ cup blackstrap molasses
   ¼ cup vegetable oil
   2 cups hot water
   3 cups whole rye flour
   3–3½ cups unbleached white flour
For Greasing:
   melted butter or margarine
Equipment:
   mixing bowl, mixing spoon or whisk, kneading board,
   3 baking pans 8″ × 4″ × 2″, plastic wrap

Mixing

Into a mixing bowl combine **2 tablespoons of yeast, 1
tablespoon of salt, ⅓ cup of blackstrap molasses, ¼ cup of
vegetable oil,** and **2 cups of hot water.** Stir.
   Add **3 cups of whole rye flour** and mix in.
   Add **2 cups of white flour,** and mix that in.

Kneading

Spread **another cup of white flour** over the kneading board
and scrape the dough out onto it. Knead it.
   Add as much of the remaining ½ **cup of white flour** as
is necessary to make the dough stop sticking (as little
as possible).
   When the dough stops sticking, knead for another 10
minutes. The dough will be quite cohesive and gets quite
springy as it approaches readiness.

Shaping the Loaves

As with the other Refrigerator Rise Breads, *this bread gets
no rise in the bowl.*
   When sufficently kneaded, divide the dough ball into
three equal parts and shape each part into a loaf to fit an
8″ × 4″ × 2″ loaf pan.
   Grease the three loaf pans with melted butter or margarine, and put a loaf into each.
   With your fingers, level out the top of each loaf.

Now, take three pieces of greased plastic wrap and cover each pan. Grease the whole piece of plastic—the bread will fall if the plastic sticks. Don't make the plastic taut and don't try to fasten it to the sides; you want it movable, to rise as the dough rises.

Rising

When the loaves are covered, set them in the refrigerator, in a place where they won't have to be moved around, and where they will have room to rise well above the pans. (Remember, don't poke the breads—pokes will stay in the loaf, even if they don't punch the dough down.)

Allow to rise in the fridge for 5–24 hours. (The last time I baked this bread I took the loaves from the fridge after 6 hours and they were beautifully risen.)

Baking

When you want to bake them, take the loaves from the refrigerator, gently remove the plastic wrap, and bake immediately in an oven set for 350°–375° (medium flame) for about 45 minutes.

Knife-test for doneness (see pp. 21–23).

Cool on a wire rack, and by all means try it warm.

Options

☞ Again, you can use **any liquid** for the water in the recipe. Try **skim milk powder** (⅔ of a cup)—just add it to the recipe after the water—or substitute **whole milk,** heated. Any **vegetable water** is a welcome addition; if it's salty, reduce the salt in the recipe. Or any combination of these. Just because you use salty vegetable water doesn't mean you can't use milk powder in the same batch, and so on.

☞ **Caraway, fennel,** or **anise seeds** are an interesting addition to any Rye Bread. You can add a tablespoon to the mixing bowl, or knead in a teaspoon per loaf when shaping the loaves.

☞ By all means substitute some **bran** or **wheat germ** for some of the rye flour.

REFRIGERATOR RYE—SUMMARY

A. 2 tbsp. active dry yeast
   1 tbsp. sea salt
   ⅓ cup blackstrap molasses
   ¼ cup vegetable oil
   2 cups hot water

B. 3 cups rye flour

C. 3–3½ cups white flour

Combine A into a bowl.

Add B, and mix in.

Add 2 cups of C, and mix in.

Spread another cup of C over kneading board, scrape batter from bowl, and knead in.

Knead in as much of remaining ½ cup as necessary to stop sticking.

Knead for 10 minutes more.

Divide into three loaves.

Grease three baking pans, 8″ × 4″ × 2″, and set a loaf in each.

Cover the pans with greased plastic wrap and set in refrigerator to rise for 5–24 hours.

When risen, gently remove plastics, and bake about 45 minutes at 350°–375°.

Knife-test for doneness. Eat warm.

PUMPERNICKEL

This traditional bread is of German origin and combines rye, whole wheat, and white flours in a chewy, flavorful loaf. Occasionally you will see "pumpernickel flour" on sale. That's a laugh; there's no such thing. It will be a mixture of two or more kinds of flour. A particular favorite with my students, Pumpernickel requires a good deal of kneading, which makes it another "friend bread."

By way of getting a "black" peasant bread, there are recipes that call for burnt crumbs mashed up in the dough (to me they just taste burnt), others that call for chocolate, still others that use chemical colorings.

We'll use blackstrap molasses and Postum (or instant coffee). Postum, for those of you who don't know it, is a coffee substitute, a roasted cereal beverage with no caffeine, but with a taste and look close to coffee (though it does contain sugar). We'll also use it for the glaze, to finish the dark color. But you are welcome to try roasted chicory or coffee for the same effect.

Pumpernickel loaves are generally free-standing, either oval or round, but if you prefer a loaf pan, there's no reason you shouldn't try it.

PUMPERNICKEL

For the Dough:
    3 tbsp. active dry yeast
    2 tsp. sea salt
    ¼ cup blackstrap molasses
    1 tbsp. Postum (or instant coffee powder)
    2 cups hot water
    ¼ cup vegetable oil
    2 cups whole rye flour
    2 cups whole wheat flour
    1–2 cups unbleached white flour
For Greasing:
    melted butter or margarine
    white cornmeal
For Glaze:
    1 tsp. Postum
    2 tsp. water
Equipment:
    large mixing bowl, mixing spoon or whisk, kneading board, 2 baking sheets, pastry brush (optional)

Mixing

Combine in your large mixing bowl **3 tablespoons of yeast, 2 teaspoons of salt, ¼ cup of blackstrap molasses, 1 tablespoon of Postum,** and **2 cups of hot water.** Stir, mixing it all together.

Mix in **¼ cup of vegetable oil.**

Add **2 cups of whole rye flour,** and mix it in.

Add **2 cups of whole wheat flour,** and mix it in.

Kneading

Spread **1 cup of white flour** over the kneading board, scrape the batter out onto the board, and knead.

Add as much of the remaining **1 cup of white flour** as necessary to stop the dough from sticking—though, remember, this is mostly a whole grain bread, and it will always be stickier than an all-white bread.

Knead for 15 minutes more.

First Rise

When kneaded (and you should see those wrinkles), drip a few drops of oil into the bowl; drop the dough ball in; turn it to oil all surfaces; cover with a clean, hot, wet towel; and set in a very warm, draft-free place to rise (about 1–1½ hours).

You can use the finger test on this dough—it's mostly wheat and has plenty of gluten and lots of elasticity.

Shaping the Loaves

When risen, punch down in the bowl, and knead for a moment to get out the larger air bubbles.

Dump the dough onto the kneading board, and cut into three pieces.

Shape each piece into a loaf, either round or oval.

Grease two large baking sheets with melted butter or margarine, and sprinkle on some **white cornmeal.**

Place two loaves on one sheet (leaving plenty of room for rising) and one loaf on the other.

Cover with a clean, dry towel, and set again in that warm, draft-free place to rise. (You'll notice that we don't slash or prick our Pumpernickel loaves. We want them to be dense.)

When the loaves are well-risen (½–¾ hour), brush the top surfaces with a **glaze** made from **1 teaspoon of Postum** dissolved in **2 teaspoons of water.** You can use your fingers or a pastry brush, but, either way, be careful not to punch the loaf down, as you'll just have to reshape and wait for it to rise again.

Baking

Bake in a moderate oven (350°–375°) for 50 minutes to 1 hour. If the loaves seem close to scorching after 50 minutes, but still test raw, shut the oven off for the last 10 minutes of baking.

The knife test for doneness isn't fully reliable for this

Rye Bread, so thump the bottom for that telltale hollow sound.

Allow to cool on a wire rack, and eat warm.

Pumpernickel is a good keeper.

Options

☞ I like to use seeds in my Pumpernickel, a tablespoon of either **caraway, anise, dill,** or **fennel,** tossed into the mixing bowl after the water, or a teaspoon of any seed kneaded into each loaf when you're shaping it. You may want to make one loaf without seeds and two with, just to see what you like.

☞ Again, you can substitute *any* liquid for the water in this recipe: **milk, beer, vegetable water,** what have you. If you want to use **skim milk,** add ⅔ cup of instant powder (⅓ cup of non-instant) right after the hot water.

☞ **Raw wheat germ** or **bran** can be substituted for part of all three flours (¼ cup of raw wheat germ and/or bran substituted for ¼ cup of each flour).

☞ **Rye meal** is especially recommended as a substitute for the rye flour in this bread. It makes the texture even more interesting.

☞ If you forget to glaze the loaf before baking, you can glaze it any time—up to and including the moment you take it from the oven. However, if you glaze it after taking the bread from the oven, the taste of the Postum is recognizable as Postum; the flavor disappears in the baking.

☞ **Yellow cornmeal** instead of white is fine for sprinkling too.

PUMPERNICKEL—SUMMARY

A. 3 tbsp. active dry yeast
   2 tsp. sea salt
   ¼ cup blackstrap
   molasses
   1 tbsp. Postum (or
   instant coffee)
   2 cups hot water

B. ¼ cup vegetable oil

C. 2 cups whole rye
   flour
   2 cups whole wheat
   flour

D. 1–2 cups unbleached
   white flour
   1 tsp. Postum in 2
   teaspoons water

Combine A into a large mixing bowl.

Mix in B.

Mix in C, 2 cups at a time.

Spread 1 cup of D over kneading board, scrape batter onto board, and knead in.

Knead in as much of the remaining cup as required to make the dough stop sticking.

Knead for an additional 15 minutes.

In the same mixing bowl, oil the dough, cover with a clean, wet towel, and set to rise in a warm, draft-free place for 1–1½ hours.

Finger-test.

Punch down, knead for a moment, then dump the dough onto the kneading board.

Cut into three pieces, and shape each piece into a loaf.

Grease two baking sheets with **melted butter** or **margarine** and **sprinkle with white cornmeal.**

Lay the loaves on the sheets, leaving room for the rise.

Cover with a clean, dry towel, and let rise for 30–45 minutes in that warm, draft-free place.

When risen, glaze with **1 teaspoon of Postum** dissolved in **2 teaspoons water.**

Bake for 50 minutes to 1 hour at 350°–375°.

Thump bottom of loaf and listen for hollow sound indicating doneness.

Cool on a wire rack. Eat warm.

☞ 8 ☜
Challah
and
Brioches:
The
Great
Egg
Breads

These oily-eggy breads are incredibly easy to handle. That's probably what inspired the French to shape theirs into a crown or topknot, and the Jews to braid theirs into Challah—because with these doughs you can! Brioche dough is even oilier than Challah, though they share a delightfully silky look and feel.

CHALLAH—THE GREAT BRAID

If you were to poll the students in my baking classes, Challah would come out in front by far.

Challah is the traditional braided Jewish Sabbath loaf. This yeast bread, rich with eggs and oil, is delicious cooled, but even better eaten warm from the oven, with pieces torn rather than cut from the loaf.

The Challah one sees in bakeries is most often made from six strands of dough (one quarter of the mixture made into a small braid of three strands, set atop a larger braid of three strands made from the remaining three quarters of the dough). But to have a loaf symbolic of the Sabbath, you need a seven-strander (one strand for each day of the week), made up of a small three atop a large three, interwoven or crowned by a single strand, signifying the Sabbath—the crown of the week.

However, the number of strands do not affect the flavor and texture of this very satisfying bread. You might want to make three- or four- or six-strand braids during the week, and bake a seven-strander Friday to greet the Sabbath on Friday night.

Challah dough is a pleasure to handle. The combination of oil and eggs gives it a feel that some students have compared to a baby's bottom and others to a woman's breast—indicating the kind of rapture experienced kneading and braiding Challah.

This bread slices beautifully when cold, and makes the best toast and French toast I know. Also, it's a fine keeper, so you don't have to be afraid of having an extra loaf around for a few days.

CHALLAH

> For the Braids:
> 2 tbsp. active dry yeast
> 4 tsp. sea salt
> ¾ cup honey
> 1¾ cups hot tap water
> 2 cups unbleached white flour (more to come)
> 1¼ cups vegetable oil
> 3 large eggs
> 5–6 more cups unbleached white flour
> For the Glaze:
> 1 egg
> poppy seeds
> For Greasing:
> melted butter or margarine
> Equipment:
> large bowl, mixing spoon or wire whisk, kneading board (if you have a marble slab—great), large baking sheet (or 2 small ones)

Mixing

Measure the **yeast, salt, honey,** and **hot water** into the bowl and stir.

Mix in the first **2 cups of flour.** (All egg breads take

part of the flour early to give the eggs something to hold onto.)

Mix in the **oil** and **3 large eggs**.

Kneading

Add **4 more cups of flour** gradually. As soon as working with the spoon or whisk becomes heavy going, clean it into the bowl (see p. 23) and switch to mixing the flour in with your bare hands. (You've begun kneading right in the bowl.) This dough is easy to knead because it is soft and yielding.

Dump the dough out onto your floured kneading board (a rubber spatula will be handy in scraping out the sides of the bowl) and knead in some of the **remaining flour**. *Don't force in every last bit of flour* that you can—this dough *must remain silky*. Because Challah dough is oilier than most that you've been used to handling, the temptation is to force in more flour to make the dough conform to what you're used to. *Don't*. Challah is a nonconformist.

Of course the exact amount of flour you use will vary from day to day, especially depending on the moisture in the air. So, if the dough is still *sticky* (not oily, but actually sticking to your fingers) when you total 8 cups of flour, all right—add a bit more. And if you've reached a cohesive ball after only 6½ cups, stop! Baking is such an inexact craft.

After all the flour is in, 8–10 minutes more kneading should bring out those faint, satiny wrinkles on the surface.

First Rise

Put your ball of kneaded dough into a greased bowl; turn it over (to grease all sides), cover with a clean towel, and let stand in a very warm place for about a 1-hour rise.

After an hour, finger-test for sufficient rise (see p. 54). Don't go by its looks in the bowl because Challah more than doubles its volume. It can fill your bowl and still not be ready. If your finger test is at all doubtful, let it rise longer: a *full* first rise is vital to light Challah.

When the rising is complete, punch down, turn the dough out onto your board and knead for a couple of minutes to get rid of the larger gas bubbles—you can feel them pop as you squeeze the dough.

If you are working on marble you may not have to flour at all, but if you are using a wooden kneading board, *flour very lightly.*

Flour your hands as little as possible for this kneading and for the shaping. The oiliness of the dough takes care of most of the sticking.

Braiding

Cut your mound of dough in half for the two loaves. (It's fun to let husband, friend, child, or visitor shape one loaf while you do the other. One teacher has her five-year-old

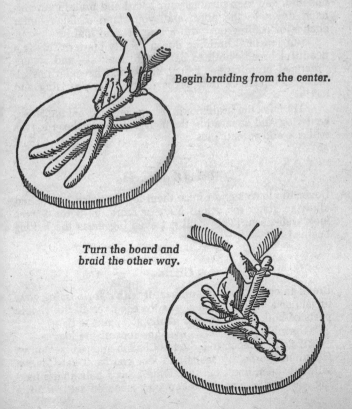

Begin braiding from the center.

Turn the board and
braid the other way.

group help her with Challah: the dough is that easy to handle.) Now, for a three-strand braid, cut the dough for your loaf into three equal lumps. Using your hands and gravity (do not roll on the board), squeeze and roll each of the three lumps of dough into a rope about an inch thick (the length of the loaf depends, of course, on the thickness of the ropes), laying them parallel on the board to be braided. (If you've never braided anything before, take a piece of string and practice.)

Begin braiding in the middle. If you start at one end you are likely to have fat ropes at the beginning and then end with them getting thinner and thinner. By starting your braid in the middle and braiding overhand down to one end, and then turning your board and braiding underhand down to the other end, you stand a much better chance of coming out with a symmetrical loaf.

But lopsided braiding doesn't really matter. This is a beautiful bread—both to eat and to look at—and an unpracticed braiding can't hurt it. In fact, irregularities almost disappear as the loaves expand during rising and baking.

Transfer the braids onto a large greased baking sheet, centering and separating them. Leave room: these loaves will rise and spread a lot.

Rising the Loaves

Cover the loaves and return them to that warm place, and allow to stand for a half hour or more, until the loaves look well-risen. (They will get even bigger as the baking begins.)

Glazing

Break an egg into a cup and beat it with a fork. Using your fingers or a pastry brush smear the egg over all the visible parts of both loaves (smear gently so as not to dent).

Sprinkle **poppy seeds** over the tops of the loaves.

If you've begun to bake the Challah and realize you've forgotten the poppy seeds and feel you can't eat Challah without them, don't despair. Even after a half hour's baking, the loaves can be taken out, smeared with a little more egg, and seeded (but do it quickly—the heat of the hot loaf will soon dry out the new glaze).

Baking

Egg Breads should bake low and slow. This one will go 50 minutes to an hour in the middle of a medium-low oven —about 350°.

If your oven—like mine and like most—gives uneven heat, turn the loaves back to front after about 40 minutes.

Use any of the standard tests for doneness (see pp. 21–23), especially a toothpick through any crack in the top, but bottom color is quite useful here—it should be a rich, almost reddish, brown. If you dripped when applying the glaze, use a metal spatula or a large-bladed knife to unseal the loaves from the baking sheet so you can take a look. (Looking at the color of the top is almost useless—the egg glaze makes the top look beautiful before it's really ready.)

Remove the loaves and stand them on a wire rack to cool. If you want to eat the Challah hot, tear chunks off the loaf. It's a poor slicer when hot—but slices well once it has cooled.

Option

☞ For a healthier loaf, substitute **1 cup or 1½ cups of raw wheat germ** for an equal amount of flour. With a cup of wheat germ in it your loaf will still be fluffy light and the flavor will be faintly *nuttier*, which most people like better.

Hints

☞ Don't skimp on the kneading just because the dough feels so nice so quickly.

☞ If the day is really damp—if it's raining now or has recently rained long and hard—decrease the water in the recipe by ⅛ cup or so. Otherwise, the loaf will accept extra flour and could come out a bit dry and less sweet.

☞ Make the braids up as soon as you have squeezed out the ropes. Otherwise, the strands tend to dry and come apart in the baking. However, if you do have to answer the phone, for instance, while braiding, and don't want to knead up the whole batch to shape anew when you come back, moisten your fingertips with water and lightly wet the ropes, especially the ends where you seal them together.

CHALLAH—SUMMARY

A. 2 tbsp. active dry yeast   C. 1¼ cups oil
   4 tsp. sea salt   3 eggs
   ¾ cup honey
   1¾ cups hot water   D. 5–6 cups flour
                              1 egg
B. 2 cups flour   poppy seeds

Measure A into a bowl, and stir.
Mix in B.
Stir in C.
Add enough D to lose stickiness, and begin kneading in bowl.
Dump dough onto board, and work into a silky texture.
Replace in oiled bowl; cover. Rise in a warm spot for about 1 hour.
Finger-test.
Punch down and knead briefly.
Braid into two loaves. Place on greased baking sheet.
Rise, covered, in warm spot for a half hour.
Glaze with **whole egg** and sprinkle on **poppy seeds**.
Bake low and slow—50 minutes to an hour at 350°.
Check doneness by bottom color and by toothpick.

BRIOCHES—THE HEAD AND THE CROWN

The word "brioche" describes a dough—made here with eggs, oil, yeast, honey, and flour, much like the Challah just made—but it also describes the various breads made from that dough: *Petites Brioches* (the small Brioche Rolls that are the most popular), *Brioche à Tête* (the head— a large, round loaf with a topknot, the same shape as the Brioche Rolls), and *Brioche Couronne* (the Crown Brioche). They are all made from the same recipe, and vary only in their shaping.

Imagine a bread lighter than Challah, with a pastry-like texture, a crisp crust that literally melts as you chew it, and a taste that has to be experienced to be believed. If the French have Brioches for breakfast every day, it's a wonder that any Frenchman gets to work on time.

There has grown up around Brioches the idea that this is the most advanced kind of bread you can make (and then only after years of practice) and that it requires two days of preparation. Well, don't you believe it! Brioches, in addition to being among the best of breads, are also among the easiest:

—they *don't* take special handling (in fact, the egg and oil make the dough *easier to handle*)

—the dough does *not* have to be refrigerated overnight (though it can be—even over several nights—without losing a bit of its texture)

—the shaping is as simple as making mudpies

—you can do *all* your kneading right in the bowl.

Brioche Rolls cook up perfectly well in muffin trays, though if you have tart molds (the kind with fluted sides), the flutings add character to the shape. If you have neither muffin pan nor tart molds, individual jello molds will do, also. (My husband and I collect agateware and we picked up a tray perfect for Brioche Rolls: shallower than the jello molds, the indentations are fluted and rounded, giving the underside of the rolls a delightful shape while the enameled iron makes for a deliciously crisp crust. The tray holds six—a morning's restrained indulgence.)

The dough keeps refrigerated for several days in a covered bowl, so don't feel you have to make the whole batch at one go. Also, they're so high in calories that a few at a time is plenty.

The texture of Brioche dough is similar to that of Challah, but it is considerably oilier and yellower in color due to the higher proportion of eggs. This oily-egginess leads to a caution: *don't flour your hands when you're handling the dough*—whether it's shaping the rolls or crown or topknot, or working out the air bubbles the next day after refrigeration—the additional flour will coarsen the texture.

This recipe makes enough for 24 Brioche Rolls or two Topknots or one or two Crowns.

You don't have to be French to be *fou* about Brioches.

BRIOCHES

For the Brioche:
  2 tbsp. active dry yeast
  ¼ cup honey
  1 tsp. sea salt
  ½ cup hot water
  ½ cup skim milk powder
  1 cup unbleached white flour (more to come)
  1 cup oil
  4½ large eggs (4 whole eggs plus 1 egg white)
  4 more cups unbleached white flour (approximately)
For the Glaze:
  1 egg yolk
Equipment:
  large bowl, wire whisk or spoon, muffin pan or tart
  molds for *Petites Brioches;* large baking sheet or molds
  for *Brioche à Tête* or *Couronne*

Mixing

Measure the **yeast, honey, salt,** and **water** into the bowl,
and stir.

Mix in the **milk powder** and **1 cup of flour.**

Add the **oil** and **4½ eggs.** (Reserve the odd yolk for
the glaze.) Beat in until smooth. Eggs and oil should be at
room temperature.

Begin to stir in the remaining **4 cups of flour.**

Kneading

When using the whisk becomes too much like work, push
the dough out from the whisk and work with your bare
hands (see p. 23).

At no point is it necessary to flour your hands. Do
not turn out onto a kneading board; the texture of Brioche
dough makes it ideal for kneading in the bowl.

Knead in flour until your kneading hand (or hands)
is cleaned by the dough and the dough shapes readily
into one large ball. *Then add no more flour.* Continue to
knead until the dough wrinkles—about 10 minutes.

First Rise

Brioche is so oily in itself that it would be superfluous to
oil the bowl, so just cover the bowl with a clean towel,

and put in a very warm place to rise for about 1½ hours. This one is the best riser in the book, practically tripling, so don't be fooled by having it apparently "doubled in bulk"; finger-test (see p. 54).

Punch down when done, and knead for a minute— enough to get the dough down to its original size.

Shaping

PETITES BRIOCHES—BRIOCHE ROLLS
This dough will make 24 Brioche Rolls.

Brioche dough is so oily that greasing the muffin tray is unnecessary.

Petites Brioches. *Fold dough to get smooth balls.*

Wet balls with one finger and place little heads with the other hand.

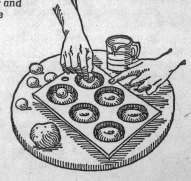

Do not flour your hands. It would be impossible to keep them floured and the oily-egginess prevents your hands from sticking.

Pinch off bits of dough and shape balls about 1½ inches in diameter. The balls are shaped by a stretching and folding or tucking motion (stretch the dough smooth across the top, and then tuck the ends into the bottom), repeated until the ball is smooth to the eye, with the rough ends pinched together at the bottom. Place a ball, smooth side up, into the depressions of your muffin tray or tart molds, and dent the tops with a finger.

Pinch off smaller bits of dough and similarly shape into ¾-inch balls, and place in the dents.

When you have finished the whole tray, wet a finger with water, lift up each smaller ball, and wet the depression—replacing the ball on the wet spot. The wet acts as a glue to keep these little heads on.

BRIOCHE À TÊTE—THE HEAD OR TOPKNOT

Divide the dough in half. (This dough will make two topknots, but I'll describe the making of one with half the dough.)

Reserve about a fifth of the lump, and with the remaining four fifths shape a ball as described for *Petites Brioches* (the topknot and the rolls have exactly the same shape—their only difference is size), stretching the dough across the top and tucking under the bottom. You can get a smooth side to begin with by folding the dough in half. Because this is a much larger dough ball, it will take more stretching and tucking.

Place the ball, smooth side up, on an ungreased baking sheet.

Shape the reserved fifth into a smaller ball, using the same method. Wet two fingers and make a depression in the center of the larger ball. Place the smaller ball into that depression.

BRIOCHE COURONNE—THE CROWN

This dough is enough for one huge crown or for two moderate crowns.

Using the same stretching and tucking method described above, shape a large ball and poke your finger

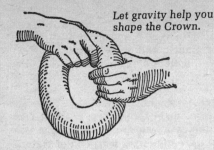

Let gravity help you
shape the Crown.

Scissoring the top of
the Couronne

through it (the poke goes through from the smooth top
to the pinched bottom).

With gravity as a stretching aid, shake the dough and
rotate the circle in your hands, forcing in more fingers, to
enlarge the hole, until the crown has an outside diameter
of about 8 inches, tucking under and pinching together
on the bottom as needed.

Place the crown on a baking sheet or in a tube pan
(if you are using an angel-food mold, the Brioche should
fill it one third or less), and make your final pulls and
pokes and tucks to get it into a fairly uniform shape.

With a pair of scissors, clip 8 to 12 slashes evenly
into the sides, about a third of the way through. This will
encourage the crown to rise out. If you want it to rise
up, clip the top.

Final Rising

Cover rolls, topknot, and/or crown and leave in a warm place to rise again for about 40 minutes. You'll see how much they swell—they'll double *before baking*.

Glazing

Break the **egg yolk** and gently spread it over the Brioches with your fingers or with a pastry brush. (If this seems too thick, you can thin the yolk with a teaspoon of water.)

Baking

Bake in a moderate (350°–375°) oven: 30–40 minutes for *Couronne* or *Brioche à Tête*; 20–25 minutes for *Petites Brioches*. The *Couronne* or the *Brioche à Tête* should be deep brown on the bottom when done; the *Petites Brioches* should range from golden to red brown. But test by sticking a toothpick into the neck or a slash.

Cool on a rack or eat them right from the muffin pans.

Although other breads, if refrigerated, would go stale (see Appendix A, pp. 191–195), the oiliness of Brioches makes it possible and in fact desirable (to avoid rancidity) to refrigerate them.

Options

☞ A **half cup of whole milk** can be substituted for the milk powder and water.

☞ Or **2 tablespoons of cream,** and milk to fill $\frac{1}{2}$ cup, can be substituted.

☞ The **grated peel of 1 lemon** gives Brioche dough an even lovelier aroma: the lemon doesn't come out lemony, it makes for a brighter flavor.

(Whenever you finish a lemon, throw the peel—pulp and all, but no seeds—into the freezer; they are so much easier to grate while still frozen.)

☞ For a healthier Brioche, you can substitute up to **1 cup of raw wheat germ** for an equal amount of flour. But in this case you do need to grease the pans, molds, or sheets before baking: the flecks of wheat germ tend to stick.

Hints

☞ For a crustier bottom use some heavier material than lightweight aluminum for baking the rolls.

☞ The *Petites Brioches* can also be baked on a baking sheet—but they will spread and won't rise as high.

☞ When eggs are dear, you can make a good Brioche with as few as 3 eggs (and then glaze with melted butter).

☞ When you break the eggs, do use your fingers to scoop out the white that clings to the shell. It is the white of the egg that has the rising power. If you leave a quarter of the white in the shell, you won't get as high results.

☞ If you are planning to refrigerate your entire batch of Brioche dough overnight, use only 1 tablespoon of yeast. Even in the fridge the yeast plants are increasing and the overnight rise in the fridge becomes equivalent to the second tablespoon of yeast. If you begin with two yeasts, your bowl of dough may push its cover off.

☞ You can do a large topknot in a mold, but let it be a high-sided mold—this one really expands. Let your dough fill less than half the mold. (If you have nothing better, try a 2-pound coffee can.)

☞ And, yes, of course you can braid it, bake it in shaped pans, or put it on a sheet in *whatever new shape you wish to invent.*

BRIOCHES—SUMMARY

A. 2 tbsp. active dry yeast
 ¼ cup honey
 1 tsp. sea salt
 ½ cup hot water

B. ½ cup skim milk powder
 1 cup flour (more to
  come)

C. 1 cup oil
 4½ eggs (4 whole
  eggs plus 1 white)

D. 4 more cups flour
  (approximately)
 1 egg yolk

Measure A into the bowl, and stir.
Mix in B.
Add C, reserving the odd yolk for the glaze, and beat till smooth.

Gradually add in D until dough is cohesive.

Knead for about 10 minutes in the bowl.

Rise for about 1½ hours in a very warm place. Finger-test.

Punch down and knead down to original size.

Shape Brioches as given on pp. 157–159.

Rise again for about 40 minutes.

Glaze with egg yolk.

Bake *Couronne* or *Brioche à Tête* 30–40 minutes at 350°–375°; bake *Petites Brioches* 20–25 minutes at the same temperature.

Toothpick-test for doneness.

9

Pizza,
Pitta,
and
Nan

Pizza, Pitta, and Nan—as marvelous a trio as you'll meet anywhere.

This is an international group of breads covering almost half the globe.

Pizza, of course, is the most western of the three, native to Italy but quite at home all over the United States.

Pitta is Middle Eastern, and can be found (with various spellings) in many countries of the Arabic world, and in Greece and Armenia, though its popularity here is growing.

Nan is pretty much of a newcomer in the States (though very popular in India, its home), but delicious and different.

All three are easier to make than you'd ever think, and all three are guaranteed to elicit the warmest compliments.

There is one trait they all share which may be a bit of a drawback in the warmer months (though more likely with Pitta and Nan than with Pizza)—they like to work in hot ovens: around 450°. Pizza takes only about 20–25 minutes and you open the oven once—to put on the filling. But the other two demand that you stay by the oven, putting in and taking out—and that can be warm work.

These are the only breads in the book for which you must preheat your oven—with Pizza, Pitta, and Nan you just don't want the slow rise that a cold oven gives.

PIZZA

The Pizza we know in America isn't *the* Pizza, but *a* Pizza, because *pizza* is an Italian word for anything that is flat and round and baked—like a pie. So, anything you want to bake flat and round—and anything you want to put on top of it—*that's* Pizza.

After saying which I have to laugh, because the Pizza we'll make together here looks very different from what you'll find in a pizza parlor. We can't duplicate the evenly heated stone linings of the commercial ovens, nor the 600°–650° temperatures. Can you imagine that heat in your kitchen? And, since I can't get large, round baking pans to fit my oven, our Pizza isn't round at all, but rectangular, and baked on everyday baking sheets.

Also, our crust will be thinner and crisper. And the fillings my husband makes for Pizza never see a canned tomato sauce. He makes the topping while I roll the dough—so much of baking is more fun with a friend.

(By the way, if you're tempted to spin your Pizza dough into the air like the professional Pizza twirlers, go right ahead—but it's not likely to do you, or your floor, much good. Commercial Pizza is made from a softer wheat —also a bleached *and* brominated wheat—which makes for a dough that's easier to flip, and one that's nutritionally poorer.)

My favorite Pizza topping is made of zucchini (green summer squash) and onions. I'll give you my husband's recipe after I've described making the crust. And for those of you who are more traditionally minded, his recipe for a tomato topping, too.

As for Pizza dough, I won't give you a recipe simply because I *don't use any particular recipe for the dough*. What I do is set aside a half or a third of whatever kneaded dough I'm making, and put that in the fridge to use for Pizza when I want it: Spiral Bread dough, French or Italian Bread dough, the Pitta dough in the following recipe—even Rich Whole Wheat dough.

And if I'm using a basically white dough, I always make sure I've used wheat germ in the recipe, so we're bound to get, between a healthful topping and the wheat germ, some good nutrition as well as the great goodness of the taste.

PIZZA

For the Dough:
    half of any kneaded bread recipe in the book (except
    Nan—which is too wet)
    3 tablespoons vegetable oil
Equipment:
    kneading board, rolling pin, 2 baking sheets

Mixing

A half of any of the recipes in this book (using 6 to 9 cups of flour) should give you two Pizzas in 11″ × 16″ baking sheets.

That means that, for instance, half of the French Bread recipe, put aside in the refrigerator and taken out in a week (or even later), will give you two 11″ × 16″ Pizzas. (Of course, you don't have to make up both Pizzas at once.)

Although you can make your Pizza as soon as you rise the dough, I'll assume you've been keeping the dough in the refrigerator (in a plastic-covered bowl, naturally) since you last baked (a week or so ago).

First, dig out baking sheets and rolling pin. Your hands are going to be oily, and you won't want to have to search. Also, it helps with the rolling-out if you have the baking sheet in front of you to check for size.

Take the bowl of dough out of the fridge and remove the plastic or wax paper cover. In the bowl, give a gentle kneading to get rid of any big air bubbles—just a minute or so.

Cut the dough in half, in the bowl.

(If you are making one Pizza, return half the dough to the fridge, and decrease the **oil** to 1½ tablespoons.)

Light your oven for preheating to as near 450° as it will get while you prepare the dough.

Pour **3 tablespoons of vegetable oil** (perhaps olive oil) over the two halves.

Shaping

Take one well-oiled half from the bowl and place it on your kneading board. With stiff fingers, poke it flat into a rectangle. (Notice that instead of flouring the board, we are oiling it, which has a similar slippery effect.) Now, with your rolling pin, roll the dough flat to the general shape of your baking sheet, with the dough very thin— about ⅛ inch.

When you think you have it large enough, place the inverted baking sheet over the dough, and cut out the dough a bit larger than the dimensions of the sheet (the dough will tend to shrink). Do what patching is necessary. Notice with the oiled dough how easily it handles and how readily any mends blend together.

Your dough should be so oily that you don't need to grease the baking sheet.

Transfer the rectangle to the baking sheet, folding over at the edges to fit the dough in, creating a raised edge.

Repeat the process for the second Pizza.

If there is any oil left in the bowl, smear it over the top of the dough with your fingers.

Baking

Put onto the oven racks to bake for about 15 minutes, or until the pizza shell is crisp.

Pour your favorite topping (or my favorite topping, which follows) over the baking dough, and sprinkle **a couple of tablespoons of grated Parmesan cheese** or **¼ cup of grated mozzarella** over each Pizza.

The topping should be hot, and so all you're waiting for now is for the cheese to heat. (If you've made your topping ahead of time, be sure to heat it before putting it on.)

Bake for another few minutes to melt the cheese.

A Pizza wheel (cutter) is handy for cutting, but a knife, judiciously handled, will do very well.

Eat it hot—sprinkled with ground red peppers if you like hot stuff.

ZUCCHINI TOPPING

1 large onion
2 cloves garlic
2–3 tbsp. vegetable oil
2–2½ pounds green squash
1 tbsp. dried oregano
2 tbsp. dried basil
1 tbsp. fennel seed
¼ tsp. sea salt

Cut **1 large onion** and **2 cloves of garlic** (large) into small bits.

Pour **2–3 tablespoons vegetable oil** into a large skillet (enough to cover the bottom without excess), and put the onion and garlic to sautée over a medium flame.

Wash and trim the ends of **2–2½ pounds of zucchini** and cut into ¼-inch slices. (Don't peel it!)

When the onions and garlic are browned, add the **zucchini,** the **oregano, basil, fennel seed,** and **salt,** and stir.

Cover and cook over a medium flame for about 20 minutes, stirring occasionally. (The exact cooking time will depend on the size of your skillet. If it is large enough not to pile the squash high, it will cook faster—if it's small, the zucchini will take longer. If it's too small, it won't hold all that zucchini, and you'll have to cook up your topping in two batches.)

QUICK TOMATO TOPPING

10 large, juicy tomatoes
2 tbsp. vegetable oil
1 tbsp. dried basil
2 tsp. fennel seed
½ tsp. sea salt
garlic powder

Wash the **tomatoes** and cut them into small pieces. (A hint: These don't by any means have to be hothouse or beefsteak or any other kind of expensive tomatoes. The cheapest you can get are as good as the best. Just make sure they are ripe, not green. They can even be overripe—the taste isn't noticeable after cooking.)

Pour **2 tablespoons of vegetable oil** into a large skillet, and dump the cut-up tomatoes in along with the **herbs** and **salt**. Sprinkle with **garlic powder** to taste. Stir and cover.

Cook over a *high* flame for 6 minutes (yes, that's all), lifting the cover only to mash the tomatoes into a mush after 4 or 5 minutes.

When topping the Pizza, spoon out with a slotted spoon to allow the water which has formed to stay in the skillet. This tomato water makes a great drink or a marvelous liquid for your next baking.

Either of these two Pizza toppings may be varied or combined in any way you please. So be sure to taste during the cooking—you may want to add a little salt or pepper, or your own special Italian trick.

PITTA

The word *pitta* is Greek for—you guessed it—pie!

On the streets of New York, you can buy Middle Eastern sandwiches; they consist of Middle Eastern bread (Pitta or Pita or Peda, etc.) with a few cubes of hot lamb and some cold salad.

The last time I made this bread in class, one of my students brought in falafel and houmis (the one like small vegetarian meatballs, the other a chick pea paste), the time before that a student brought Baba Ganouj (an eggplant puree) and Middle East salad.

But you don't have to eat Middle Eastern to make and enjoy Pitta. It's great just as it is, hot (and I do mean hot) from the oven, or as the bread for any sandwich—it even makes great hamburger rolls.

The greatest thing about Pitta isn't what you put into it, but the bread itself. It is tasty, crisp, with a delicious aroma.

If you've never seen Pitta, ours is a round, flat bread, about 5 inches across, that forms an internal pouch in the baking. (It's this that makes it such a natural for fillings —you just slit it open and there's a ready-made pouch waiting for *something*.) The surface should come out a golden-to-dark brown that is very attractive.

Commercial Pitta is often larger than what we bake (ours is an easy size to handle), thinner, too, but nowhere near as light or tasty.

There are certain things to watch for in making this specialty. The dough is first formed into balls and then flattened into rounds ¼ inch thick. If you leave creases in the dough as you shape the rounds, or if you pinch the dough as you shape them, these creases or pinches tend to stay, and the Pitta won't rise there. You've lost your chance of a pouch along that pinch.

You may have to flour your hands lightly when handling the dough balls for shaping—and you'll certainly have to lightly flour the kneading board where you put them to rest (the balls get a 10-minute rest before flattening).

The dough is medium-stiff: neither very stiff, like Italian Bread, nor almost wet, like French Bread.

The recipe will make a dozen Pitta, each weighing about 4 ounces before baking, if you want to check the dough balls for size.

Greeks or Armenians of the older generation make this bread directly on the bottom of the oven (understand that I don't mean the bottom rack, or under the broiler, but the metal shelf just over the flame). They will pat the balls out, and flip them onto the bottom of the oven (without any greasing) and then pull them out with a long spatula or a baker's peel.

In my city apartment, with my ancient oven, I can't bring myself to bake directly on the bottom, so we'll use a baking sheet (greased only once, before the baking) large enough to hold two Pitta at a time, and then put the sheet onto the bottom. I hope the Greeks will forgive me. If you want to try the bottom of your oven directly, and it's clean enough, there's no reason why you shouldn't.

Bottom color is the indicator for this bread. It has a tendency to go dark on the bottom, and to be completely baked, while the top is still pale. No difficulty. If the bottom shows dark, put the baking sheet under the broiler flame for half a minute or less (I do it for a counted 20 seconds!) until brown on top.

I preheat my oven only for the 10 minutes that the balls require to rest, which means the first pair takes a little longer than subsequent pairs (I bake them two at a time). The first pair bakes in about 7 minutes, the second in about 6 minutes, the subsequent ones in about 5 minutes each.

PITTA

For the Dough:
  1 tbsp. active dry yeast
  2 tbsp. honey
  1 tbsp. sea salt
  2 cups hot water
  5–6 cups unbleached white flour
For Greasing:
  melted butter or margarine
Equipment:
  large mixing bowl, mixing spoon or whisk, kneading board, baking sheet

Mixing

(If you've never made a kneaded bread before, read pp. 52–53.)

Into your mixing bowl, combine **1 tablespoon of yeast, 2 tablespoons of honey, 1 tablespoon of salt,** and **2 cups of hot tap water,** and stir.

Add the first **4 cups of flour,** 2 cups at a time, mixing in well.

Spread **1 cup of flour** over your kneading board, scrape the dough onto the board, and knead in.

Add as much of the **remaining cup of flour** as required to make up a medium-stiff dough.

Knead for a few more minutes.

First Rise

Drip a few drops of oil into the scraped-out bowl and drop the dough ball back in, turning it to oil the surface.

Cover with a clean towel, and put in a very warm, draft-free place to rise for about an hour.

When the finger test (see p. 54) shows the dough is risen, punch down and knead gently for a moment to get rid of any big bubbles.

Shaping

Dump the dough out onto your lightly floured board. Cut it into 12 roughly equal pieces. Don't try to make all the Pitta exactly the same size. If some are larger and some smaller, no harm. But if you take little bits from one and stick them onto another, the seam or crease that's left will keep the Pitta from rising along that line.

Roll the 12 pieces into 12 balls. Put each ball on the floured board. Cover the dozen with a clean towel and let rest for 10 minutes.

Preheat your oven by setting it on high. You want to bake these at about 450°, but the opening and putting in and taking out tends to keep the temperature down a bit. If yours will go to 450° and stay there, great. If your oven is like mine, set it for high, and let it stay there. If your thermometer shows your oven going much over 500°, level it off.

After 10 minutes, uncover the balls of dough and begin to shape. Pull one gently from the board, lay it on the palm of your hand, and press and pat until it begins to flatten. (If the ball wants to stick to you, flour your hands.)

Now, because the balls have rested for that 10 minutes, the tops have dried out slightly, giving them a dry side and a wet side. Lay the dry side on the board, and, with the palm of your hand, pat, press, and pound (but don't poke) until the ball is flattened into a round of dough, about ¼ inch thick and 5 inches across.

Gently lift this round of dough from the board, and lay it on the baking sheet, leaving room for another. Flatten it a little more after you've transferred it—it tends to thicken up.

Repeat for the next ball. Don't pinch or squeeze the dough too thin. It won't rise where it's pinched.

Flatten only two at a time—and only when you're ready to put them on the sheet. Made even a few minutes in advance, the rounds will begin to rise and be difficult to handle.

Baking

Put the baking sheet on the bottom of the oven, and bake for 5-7 minutes, or until the bottom color shows dark brown (lift the "pie" with a spatula or pancake turner, and peek).

If the top color is pale, put under the broiler for a few seconds, until brown.

Dump the finished Pitta onto a plate for serving straight from the oven, and begin to flatten your next pair. I told you that you'd be busy at the oven!

If wanted for sandwiches, slit one side and insert the filling.

PITTA—SUMMARY

A. 1 tbsp. active dry yeast   B. 5–6 cups flour
   2 tbsp. honey
   1 tbsp. sea salt
   2 cups hot water

Combine A into a bowl and stir.

Add the first 4 cups of B, 2 cups at a time.

Spread another cup (no. 5) over kneading board and scrape dough onto flour. Knead in.

Add as much of another cup as required to knead up a medium-stiff dough.

Drip a few drops of oil into the bowl and drop in dough, oiling all surfaces.

Cover with a clean towel, and set in a warm, draft-free place to rise for about 1 hour.

Finger-test.

Punch down and knead out large air bubbles.

Roll into 12 balls, and place the balls on the lightly floured board.

Light oven, set for 450°.

Cover balls and rest them for 10 minutes.

After 10 minutes, flatten two balls into rounds about $\frac{1}{4}" \times 5"$.

Lay rounds on a greased baking sheet (flatten a little more) and bake on the bottom of the oven until bottom of Pitta shows dark brown.

Brown tops under broiler for a few seconds.

Remove from oven and start flattening the next pair.

Serve very hot.

NAN

I don't know any Hindi but I can't help wondering if nan means pie. Nan is by far the tastiest of this trio (at least as far as the dough itself—I make no comparison between any bread and my husband's good Pizza topping). But, like many beautiful creatures, you have to know how to handle her. Nan is worked with a dough that is almost too wet to handle. What happens is that we mix up a dough that never does get enough flour in to stop sticking to your hands while you're kneading, but which, after being left to rise for about an hour, pulls itself together enough to be just handleable—with floured hands and board.

Like Pitta, this dough is separated into small balls before being flattened into shape. Like Pitta and Pizza, it is baked in a preheated oven around 450°.

Unlike Pitta, this flat bread is not expected to make its own pocket or pouch in the baking. Nor is it used like Pitta as a sandwich of sorts (though it can be). Nan is a dinner bread, brought to the table hot and eaten with the meal—but I find it crisp and delicious enough to have with a cup of tea instead of a sweet roll.

I hope all your burns are healing well from our baking of Pitta, for the same cautions apply here. We'll be opening and closing the oven, putting baking sheets in and taking them out, so be sure you have adequate potholders.

We'll knead and rise Nan in its mixing bowl, but we'll have need of the board later, so be sure it's handy.

Nan is not a beginner's first bread—at least I don't think of it as simple. My recommendation would be to get the feel of a couple of other kneaded breads before you tackle Nan.

When kneading, use only the fronts of your fingers—don't dig in as you would with other, drier doughs. And use only one hand to knead. You're going to require the other hand clean and dry to get you out of the sticky dough and add more bits of flour as you knead. Just push the dough around for a while—until you see the sheeting that we spoke of in Method Breads (see p. 31): that elasticity that shows gluten development. Remember, flour your hands as you work—and when you get to the board, flour your hands and the board.

NAN

For the Dough:
   1 tbsp. active dry yeast
   1 tbsp. honey
   2 tsp. sea salt
   $\frac{1}{4}$ cup vegetable oil
   $\frac{1}{4}$ cup yogurt or buttermilk
   1 egg
   1 cup hot water
   $3\frac{1}{4}$–4 cups unbleached white flour
For Greasing:
   melted margarine or butter
For Glaze:
   melted margarine or butter
   poppy seeds
Equipment:
   mixing bowl, mixing spoon or whisk, kneading board
   or platter, baking sheet, pastry brush

Mixing

Into a mixing bowl measure **1 tablespoon of yeast, 1 ta-blespoon of honey, 2 teaspoons of salt, $\frac{1}{4}$ cup of vegetable oil** (sesame oil gives a nice Oriental touch), and **$\frac{1}{4}$ cup of yogurt** or buttermilk. Stir together.

Mix in **1 large egg.**

Add **1 cup hot tap water,** and stir everything together.

Mix in the **first 3 cups flour,** a cup at a time.

Flour your hand, and add more flour, a little at a time, kneading in the bowl, until the dough begins to show the first signs of not sticking. You should be kneading with only one hand, and not really digging in, but rather pushing the dough around with the flats of your fingers.

From time to time clean your hand off with a scraper or spoon (and re-flour), because dough tends to stick to dough.

At somewhere past $3\frac{1}{4}$ cups of flour, you should be able to just handle the dough—albeit gingerly.

First Rise

Scrape the dough down off the sides of the bowl, onto the ball at the bottom. Cover with a clean towel, and set in a warm, draft-free place to rise.

The rise should take about an hour, but even here give it the finger test (see p. 54).

If it passes, flour your hand, punch it down, and knead out the bigger bubbles.

Shaping

Flour your kneading board (or a large platter—you won't be kneading, so all you require is a place big enough to set down balls of dough without their touching each other).

Scrape the dough ball out onto the floured board and cut into 12 roughly equal pieces.

With floured hands, roll each piece into a ball, and place on the floured board to rise for 10 minutes, covered with a clean towel. Don't try to make perfect balls—you're going to change the shape in 10 minutes anyhow.

Set your oven on high for preheating during the 10-minute rest.

You want to bake these little beauties (like the Pitta) at about 450°.

Grease a large baking sheet—this once for the whole batch.

Pick up your first ball (with floured hands) and flatten it between your hands to an oval shape about ¼-inch thick. Do try not to let it be thicker. If you find round loaves more attractive than irregular ovals, then just flatten the ball into a circle, but still ¼-inch thick.

Lay the oval (or circle) on the baking sheet, leaving room for one other (we bake Nan two at a time), and press it a little flatter with the flat of your hand.

Repeat the process with the second ball—flouring your hands, flattening, setting onto the baking sheet, flattening a bit more.

Dip your pastry brush into melted butter or margarine and brush the tops of the flat loaves. Sprinkle with a few poppy seeds.

Baking

As with Pitta, put the baking sheet onto the bottom of the oven (see p. 169).

The first pair can take as much as 8 minutes to bake;

the last may come out in 4½ minutes: you have to keep track of what's happening in the oven.

When the bottom color is dark brown (not golden—*dark* brown), the Nan is ready to come out. If the top is pale, as it is likely to be, then slip the baking sheet *under the broiler* for a fraction of a minute—sometimes only 10 or 20 seconds. But check: it's worth the extra effort to keep your loaves from scorching.

And do not cool.

Serve these wonderful Indian loaves as hot as you can get them to the table—two at a time. You'll seldom get bigger compliments.

NAN—SUMMARY

A. 1 tbsp. active dry yeast
   1 tbsp. honey
   2 tsp. sea salt
   ¼ cup vegetable oil
   ¼ cup yogurt or
      buttermilk

B. 1 egg

C. 1 cup hot water

D. 3¼–4 cups flour
   melted butter or
      margarine
   poppy seeds

Mix A into a large bowl.

Stir in B.

Add C and mix well.

Mix in the first three cups of D, 1 cup at a time.

Add as much more of D as required to show the first signs of not sticking, kneading in bowl, gently. (Keep hand floured during the kneading.)

Knead for a few more minutes.

Scrape down the dough, cover with a clean towel, and set in a warm, draft-free place to rise for about 1 hour.

Punch down (with floured hand) and gently press out any large air bubbles.

Shape into 12 equal balls, and place on floured kneading board.

Light oven, set for high.

Cover balls and let rest for 10 minutes.

With floured hand, shape two balls into ovals, ¼ inch thick. Lay them on greased baking sheet.

Brush tops with melted butter or margarine and sprinkle with a few poppy seeds.

Bake with sheet directly on bottom of the oven, for 5–8 minutes. Check bottom color for doneness.

Put under broiler for a few seconds to darken top color.

Serve hot from the oven.

(Repeat until all are baked.)

10

Batter
Breads

It's appropriate that the last recipes in this book should be Batter Breads as the first were Method Breads, which evolved from Batter Breads.

"Batter" is any dough that is too wet to be kneaded. With all batter breads, you could add about 25 percent more flour, and you'd be able to knead them.

Then, just what is the point of Batter Breads?

Well, these moist batters are able to carry many heavy—and delicious—ingredients that would leave any other kind of bread too dense.

Nor can these recipes be made by our much quicker Method Bread technique. We've tried, but the Cottage Casserole collapses; Rye Batter won't rise. So if you want the delicious breads of this chapter, you're going to have to use the full-rise Batter Bread technique.

We'll work through the recipes of three Batter Breads (and one variation) in this chapter. And when I say "work," I mean work.

To me, Batter Breads are more tiring than any kneaded bread—though some of my students disagree. The kneading motion is easy for me—the stirring and hand-squeezing that batters require tire me out.

But there is good reason to bake Batter Breads—if only for their high-rising lightness.

All of these breads require a similar technique: after the liquid (and most of the other ingredients) you add part of the flour, and whip it, either by hand or by mixer, to develop the gluten early. This beating is most important, because now is when the batter is easiest to work, so you get the most gluten development for your labor.

You then add the rest of the flour a bit at a time, stirring after each addition, until you reach the point where stirring by spoon is too much like work. At this point you clean the spoon off into the bowl, then work the batter by squeezing it between your fingers.

Use only one hand for squeezing; you'll want one hand clean for adding more flour (if necessary) and for scraping the batter off the working hand. This is sticky stuff.

After the flour is all in, the batter squeezed between your fingers for a few minutes, and your hand scraped clean, you put these batters to rise, just like most doughs. But don't finger-test—just *look*, as we did with Rye Breads; these too will look doubled when ready.

As for the beating times, these are flexible. If you beat as rapidly, vigorously, and continuously as my husband does, you can reduce the time. If, on the other hand, you're sitting in front of your favorite soap opera, and beating only when you think of it—you'll take much longer. My beating times are for beating, resting a few seconds, then beating again, and so on. You must judge your own batter. If it seems to lack cohesion, work it some more.

When risen, the batter will be easier to handle (though still sticky). Punch it down, and press out the bubbles. You notice that I don't say knead out. If you start kneading this bread you'll just get all over batter again. Dump the batter into a *well-greased* pan. The heavier your container (a casserole, for instance) the crisper your crust will be.

Don't overfill the containers. If you do, your bread will come out heavier than it should. Or the bread will rise too far above the sides of the container to support itself, and it may fall.

The batter should about half-fill the pan. If the recipe calls for a 1½-quart casserole, and yours is only a 1-quart-er, reserve a third of the dough and make drop rolls from it. (The rolls should bake in 20–25 minutes.)

You can substitute a soufflé dish of equal size for a casserole.

Once in, poke the batter into any and all corners, level it off, and smooth out its surface. As with Method Breads, the batter will rise and bake in whatever shape you leave it. If you leave corners unfilled, those corners will stay unfilled. If you leave one side high and one side low, the high side will be higher after baking. If you leave the surface looking like no-man's-land with foxholes and bomb craters, you'll wind up with the same uneven terrain (albeit a lovely dark brown).

If the batter still wants to stick during these pokings and proddings, just butter your hand a little, and you'll come clean. And be careful to *grease the pan generously* —Batter Breads like to stick: don't help them.

I can't emphasize too much how different and delicious these three breads are, though don't underestimate the time it takes to make them. These are by no stretch of the imagination "quick breads." They take no more preparation time than any bread (less than some), but they do, as any bread other than a Method Bread does, need their full rise.

Don't skimp on that first rise.

But don't let the second rise go too far! Once these breads are in the pan, ring, or casserole, *let the batter rise only to the lip of your container,* and then bake. (They will rise still higher in the baking—so leave room in the oven.) If you have let them rise beyond the lip, punch down and let them rise again.

If you have an electric mixer, by all means use it on the first flour: after that, the batter is too stiff (though I had a student who swore she was able to make the Cottage Casserole *all the way by mixer*).

Now that I've thoroughly intimidated you, screw your courage to the sticking place—which in this case is right in the bowl with all that batter—and let's begin.

COTTAGE CASSEROLE

This is my favorite Batter Bread, bar none.

The seeds and onion give it an eye-popping flavor, while the cottage cheese makes for unique texture.

I bake it in a 1½-quart casserole and the crust is so crisp and tasty, it's hard to imagine that this is bread and not some exotic fried dish.

You've noticed that I often give different liquids as options for the hot water in a recipe, on the theory that vegetable water or milk can be even better than plain water. Well, in this recipe, the "water" is cottage cheese. If that isn't reaching for "water" I don't know what is.

(If you want to use pot cheese or farmer cheese, which are drier, add ¼ cup of warm milk.)

The cottage cheese makes this bread tremendously high in protein, while the wheat germ adds vitamins and protein of its own. All in all, a very tasty, nutritious, attractive, and satisfying loaf. (Just add a salad and you have a complete, healthful meal.)

COTTAGE CASSEROLE

The Batter:
    1½ cups creamed cottage cheese
    1 tbsp. vegetable oil
    1½ tbsp. active dry yeast
    2 tbsp. honey
    1 tbsp. dry minced onion (or onion flakes)
    1 tbsp. dill seed
    1 tsp. sea salt
    1 large egg
    2 cups unbleached white flour
    ¼ cup raw wheat germ
For Greasing:
    melted butter or margarine
Equipment:
    large mixing bowl, strong mixing spoon, 1½-quart casserole

Mixing

In a small saucepan, heat **1½ cups of creamed cottage cheese** with **1 tablespoon of vegetable oil** to hot, not boiling. (Test with a finger.)

In your bowl, combine this mixture with **1½ tablespoons of yeast,** and mix.

Add **2 tablespoons of honey, 1 tablespoon of dry minced onion, 1 tablespoon of dill seed, 1 teaspoon of salt,** and **1 large egg** (at room temperature). Stir together until the egg yolk is all worked in.

Add **1 cup of flour** and beat in (by mixer for 2 minutes or by hand for 5 minutes).

Mix in **¼ cup of raw wheat germ** and stir for a minute by hand.

Add another **½ cup of flour,** and stir for a minute.

Add the final **½ cup of flour,** clean the batter off your

spoon into the bowl, and, with one bare hand, squeeze the batter between your fingers and stir it, working it as vigorously as you can for another 2 minutes. (If you can't work vigorously, do it gently for several minutes.)

The batter should be very cohesive. My husband made it recently, and came in to show me the batter around his hand like the "Blob," sticky enough to support the weight of the light mixing bowl.

(By the way, I hope you know where your watch and rings are—this batter can pull them right off.)

First Rise

With a spoon or scraper in your clean hand, scrape the batter from your working hand into the bowl, pushing the odd bits into the rest of the batter at the bottom of the bowl.

Set in a very warm, draft-free place to rise, wash your hands clean, then get a towel and cover the bowl.

Rising will take 50 minutes to an hour, and the batter will look doubled.

Filling the Casserole

When risen, punch down and press out the larger bubbles with your hand.

It should be easier to handle now—a rising does that for a batter or a sticky dough—but if you find it still too sticky, spread your fingers with a little melted butter or margarine.

Generously grease a 1½-quart casserole, either oval or round, and scrape the batter in, making sure to press it down into the corners, and to level off the top, and smooth the surface. For all of this, your hand is the best tool, but it could be done with a well-greased spatula.

When the batter is satisfactorily smoothed and evened and poked, re-cover with that clean towel, and set again to rise to the lip of the casserole—about half the time of the first rise.

Baking

When the batter has risen to the lip, bake in a moderately slow oven (340°–360°) for about 35–40 minutes.

Test for doneness (see pp. 21–23). Because of the cottage cheese, you're allowed a few faint streaks on the knife, even when the bread is done.

When done (the top crust will have a lovely dark-golden-brown look), turn out of the casserole carefully (that casserole is hot and dangerous), and bring right to the table.

This bread is not easily sliced when hot, but it can be torn apart with delicious results. If you insist on cutting, use a serrated knife and saw slowly and gently.

Options

☞ The **seeds** are of course variable. You might prefer **caraway** or **fennel** or **anise** or **celery seeds**.

☞ For those of you with a taste for adventure, try substituting **dry minced garlic** for the onion. I did it by accident one day, and was pleasantly surprised.

☞ If you want a topping, brush the top with melted butter or margarine as soon as the loaf is taken from the casserole, and **sprinkle** with **caraway seeds or dill** and/or **coarse salt**.

☞ You might want to substitute **bran** for the wheat germ.

COTTAGE CASSEROLE—SUMMARY

A. 1½ cups creamed cottage cheese
   1 tbsp. vegetable oil

B. 1½ tbsp. active dry yeast

C. 2 tbsp. honey
   1 tbsp. dry minced onion
   1 tbsp. dill seed
   1 tsp. sea salt
   1 large egg

D. 2 cups flour

E. ¼ cup raw wheat germ

Warm A in a saucepan.
Add to B and mix.
Stir in C until fairly smooth.
Mix in 1 cup of D and beat (with electric mixer for 2 minutes or by hand for 5).

Add E and beat for 1 minute by hand.

Add another ½ cup of D and beat for 1 minute.

Add another ½ cup of D and work with bare hand for 2 minutes.

Cover with a clean towel and rise in a warm, draft-free place until doubled (about 50 minutes to an hour).

Punch down.

Grease well a 1½-quart casserole, and put in the batter, poking into the corners and smoothing the top.

Return to a warm place, covered, and rise only until the batter reaches the lip of the casserole.

Bake at 340°–360° for 35–40 minutes.

Turn out and serve immediately. Tear apart, rather than slicing.

ANADAMA BREAD

What's more American than cornmeal? After all, corn was the one major New World grain, and all cornbreads and cornmeal breads and similar recipes are rooted in the Americas.

This is an adaptation of a very old recipe (don't ask me what Anadama means) and its main claim to fame is that it is delicious, crunchy, and nutritious.

We bake our Anadama Bread in a 9″ × 5½″ × 2¾″ baking pan, and it makes one large, beautiful loaf, all the handsomer for brushing with butter and sprinkling with cornmeal before baking.

In many cornmeal recipes, the meal is added early on, and mixed into boiling or very hot water to soften it. We prefer the crunchiness, and so add it late in the mixing.

The eggs are added after the first 2 cups of flour to give the eggs something to grab onto in the mixing. It makes for a smooth batter.

Do use 100 percent whole stone-ground cornmeal, it's so much better for you than the usual degerminated pap.

Are you ca
in the nutriti

Are you br
home less th

The real way to get the most for your money is to get the most out of your food —in nutrition and taste. Foods may look alike, may be priced alike—but there may be a big gap in their nutritional value. You may think you're buying more nutrition than you really are.

When you know what you are looking for on a label, you'll bring home a much better bag of groceries. Standard Brands Incorporated encourages it because their labels show how their emphasis has always been on your family's health and well-being. Here, and on the following pages, are just a few of the Standard Brands stories:

Delicious **Fleischmann's® Margarine** —made from 100% corn oil. So low in satu

ANADAMA BREAD

Makes 2 loaves

5½ to 6½ cups unsifted flour
2½ teaspoons salt
1 cup yellow corn meal
2 packages Fleischmann's® Active Dry Yeast
¼ cup (½ stick) softened Fleischmann's® Margarine
2 cups very hot tap water
½ cup molasses (at room temperature)

In a large bowl thoroughly mix 2½ cups flour, salt, corn meal and undissolved yeast. Add margarine.

Gradually add very hot tap water and molasses; beat 2 minutes at medium speed of electric mixer, scraping bowl occasionally. Add ½ cup flour, or enough flour to make a thick batter. Beat at high speed 2 minutes, scraping bowl occasionally. Stir in enough additional flour to make a soft dough. Turn out onto floured board; knead until smooth and elastic, about 8 to 10 minutes. Place in greased bowl; turn to grease top. Cover; let rise in warm place, until doubled in bulk, about 1 hour.

Punch dough down; turn out onto floured board. Divide in half and shape into loaves. Place in 2 greased 8¼ x 4½ x 2½-inch pans. Cover; let rise in warm place, until doubled in bulk, about 45 minutes.

Bake at 375°F. about 35 minutes, or until done. Remove from pans and cool.

ANADAMA BREAD

For the Batter:
    1 tbsp. active dry yeast
    1 cup hot water
    ⅓ cup skim milk powder
    3 tbsp. vegetable oil
    3 tbsp. blackstrap molasses
    1½ tsp. sea salt
    3½ cups unbleached white flour
    2 large eggs
    ¼ cup raw wheat germ
    ½ cup whole yellow cornmeal
For Greasing:
    melted butter or margarine
For the Crust:
    melted butter or margarine
    more cornmeal
Equipment:
    large mixing bowl, strong mixing spoon, baking pan
    (9″ × 5½″ × 2¾″)

Mixing

Into a mixing bowl measure and mix **1 tablespoon of yeast,
1 cup of hot tap water,** and **⅓ cup of skim milk powder**
(⅔ cup if non-instant).

Add **3 tablespoons of vegetable oil, 3 tablespoons of
blackstrap molasses,** and 1½ **teaspoons of salt**. Mix in.

Add the first **2 cups of flour** and beat (by hand for
5 minutes, or at low speed by mixer for 2 minutes).

Beat in **2 large eggs** (at room temperature) for another
2 minutes by hand (1 by machine).

(All the following beating times are for hand beating
—if you've a machine that will go this far, more power to
you, and it.)

Beat in, for 1 minute, ¼ **cup of raw wheat germ.**

Beat in, for 1 minute, ½ **cup of yellow cornmeal.**

Beat in, for 2 minutes, **1 more cup of flour.**

Clean your mixing spoon into the bowl, add the last
½ **cup of flour,** and work with your bare hand for 2 or 3
minutes, as vigorously as you can manage without strain.

First Rise

Scrape the batter from your hand, into the bowl, and
cover with a clean towel, to rise in a warm, draft-free
place for about 1½ hours or until doubled.

Filling the Pan

When risen, punch down, press out the larger bubbles, and dump into a 9″ × 5½″ × 2¾″ baking pan, greased with melted butter or margarine.

Even the batter in the pan, poke it into any and all corners, and smooth the surface.

Brush the top with **melted butter** or **margarine** and sprinkle with additional **cornmeal.**

Set to rise again, covered with a clean towel, in that same warm place, until the batter reaches the lip of the pan (probably less than half the time of the first rise). Make certain it rises no further before baking. If the loaf does rise much above the lip, punch it down and start the rise over again, or the bread is likely to sag in the baking and turn out heavy and disappointing.

Baking

When it has reached the lip, set the loaf to bake at 350°–375° for about 35–40 minutes.

The top will be a dark brown.

Test for doneness (see pp. 21–23).

Cool on a wire rack, but serve hot.

Options

☞ Substitute **millet meal** for cornmeal, if you wish. To me the millet gives the loaf more corn flavor than the cornmeal does.

☞ If you find this bread not sweet enough, you could substitute **honey** for the molasses, but I'd never do it.

☞ Just for a change, how about **bran** for the wheat germ?

☞ If you don't want to brush the crust with melted butter or margarine, brush with **milk** as soon as you've evened the batter in the pan, and then sprinkle with cornmeal. If you've used millet meal instead of the corn, sprinkle with **millet meal.**

☞ For even more crunch, try **cornmealing** the baking pan after greasing and before the batter goes in.

ANADAMA BREAD—SUMMARY

A. 1 tbsp. active dry yeast
    1 cup hot water
    ⅓ cup skim milk
       powder

b. 3 tbsp. vegetable oil
    3 tbsp. blackstrap
       molasses
    1½ tsp. sea salt

C. 3½ cups flour

D. 2 large eggs

E. ¼ cup raw wheat germ

F. ½ cup yellow cornmeal
       melted margarine or
          butter
       more cornmeal

Combine A into a large mixing bowl.
Stir in B.
Add 2 cups of C and beat (2 minutes by mixer, 5 by hand).
Beat in D (2 minutes by hand, 1 by mixer).
Beat in E (1 minute by hand).
Beat in F (1 minute by hand).
Beat in 1 more cup of D (2 minutes by hand).
With your bare hand, work in the last ½ cup of D, for 2 or 3 minutes.
Cover and set in a warm, draft-free place to rise for 1½ hours (until doubled).
Punch down and scrape into a 9″ × 5½″ × 2¾″ baking pan, greased with melted butter or margarine.
Re-rise until batter reaches lip of baking pan.
Bake for 35–40 minutes, 350°–375°.
Knife-test.
Cool on a wire rack.

RYE BATTER BREADS

Here's a bread that combines the flavor of rye with the coarseness of a Batter Bread.

In the development of this recipe I tried it two ways: the two were so close in popularity with my classes that I decided to give you both. I'm not generous, I just couldn't make up my mind.

First, I'll present Light Rye Batter Bread, and go through the bread with you, and then just give the recipe for Dark Rye Batter Bread, the healthier of the two—the technique is the same.

As this recipe employs rye flour, it's even stickier than the other Batter Breads. However, it's a truly hearty bread, and a treat to bring to the table.

This batter calls for a 2-quart casserole. Remember what I said about not overfilling the pans. If you have only a smaller casserole, use some of the excess for drop rolls—but don't fill the pans more than halfway.

And if the batter rises above the lip, punch it down and start the rising again. One of my students brought in a Rye Batter Bread casserole that had risen above the lip before baking, and there in the center was a lovely hole— looking like a mouse had been nibbling.

LIGHT RYE BATTER BREAD

For the Batter:
   2 tbsp. active dry yeast
   2 tbsp. caraway seeds
   2 tsp. sea salt
   ¼ cup vegetable oil
   ¼ cup honey
   1½ cups hot water
   ½ cup skim milk powder
   2 cups unbleached white flour
   2 cups rye flour
For Greasing:
   melted butter or margarine
Equipment:
   large mixing bowl, strong mixing spoon, 2-quart casserole

Mixing

Into a large mixing bowl measure **2 tablespoons of yeast, 2 tablespoons of caraway seeds, 2 teaspoons of salt;** then **¼ cup of vegetable oil** and **¼ cup of honey** (in the same measuring cup), **1½ cups of hot tap water,** and **½ cup of skim milk powder.** Stir until blended.

Mix in **2 cups of white flour,** and beat for about 5 minutes by hand. (At this point, the batter is already too stiff for my mixer.)

Mix in **1 cup of rye flour** and beat for 2 minutes.

Mix in the **last cup of rye flour,** and work with your bare hand for 3 minutes, squeezing between your fingers, and generally agitating the batter.

Batter Breads 189

First Rise

Scrape the batter off your fingers into the bowl, cover with a clean, *hot*, *wet* towel, and set in a very warm, draft-free place to rise until doubled, about 1½ hours.

Filling the Casserole

When risen, punch down and in the bowl press out any big air bubbles.

Grease well a 2-quart casserole (and I do mean *well*) and dump the batter in, poking into all the corners, even the level of the batter and smooth out its surface.

Set to rise again, covered with a clean, dry towel until the batter reaches the lip of the casserole (probably about half the time of the first rise).

Baking

When risen to the lip of the casserole, set to bake in a moderate oven, 350°–375°, for about 45–55 minutes.

Test for doneness (see pp. 21–23).

Turn out of the casserole carefully, and serve hot.

DARK RYE BATTER BREAD

For the Batter:
  2 tbsp. active dry yeast
  2 tbsp. dark caraway
  2 tsp. sea salt
  ¼ cup vegetable oil
  ¼ cup blackstrap molasses
  2 cups hot water
  ⅔ cup skim milk powder
  2½ cups unbleached white flour
  ½ cup raw wheat germ
  2¼ cups whole rye flour
  (into a 2½-quart casserole)

Options

☞ Any of the ingredients that differ in the Dark Rye recipe can be substituted in the Light Rye recipe:

dark caraway for caraway; **blackstrap** for honey; and
¼ **cup of raw wheat germ** for ½ cup of the rye flour.

☞ For a topping, just before you put the loaf to
rise, brush with **melted butter** or **margarine** and sprinkle
on **coarse salt and caraway seeds** (or dark caraway).

LIGHT RYE BATTER BREAD—SUMMARY

A. 2 tbsp. active dry yeast
    2 tbsp. caraway seeds
    2 tsp. sea salt
    ¼ cup vegetable oil
    ¼ cup honey
    1½ cups hot water
    ½ cup skim milk powder

B. 2 cups unbleached white
    flour

C. 2 cups whole rye flour

Mix A into a large bowl.

Mix in B and beat for 5 minutes by hand.

Mix in 1 cup of C and beat for 2 minutes.

Mix in last cup of C and work for 3 minutes.

Cover with a clean, hot, wet towel and rise in warm,
draft-free place until doubled (about 1½ hours).

Punch down and press out air bubbles.

Grease 2-quart casserole and put in batter, pressing
into all corners and smoothing.

Rise, covered by dry towel, until batter reaches lip of
casserole.

Bake for 45–55 minutes at 350°–375°.

Test with knife for doneness.

Serve hot.

Appendix A
Keeping
Bread
and
Dough

Between my classes and research, I bake a lot more bread than we can eat or fit in our freezer, so we give some away to neighbors—which makes for some very happy neighbors. People are not surprised that a home-baked bread tastes better than store-bought: they expect that; what does surprise them is how well these breads keep.

Actually, it's not so surprising; for one thing, home-made bread is eaten as much as a day sooner than a commercial bread would be. More important, commercial breads are kneaded in machines which force air into them (which is why so many of them seem to have no substance). This allows their bread to dry out faster.

Most important, though, we use fresher, wholesome, unchemicaled ingredients which are less likely to go stale quickly.

If commercial bakers used honey and the ingredients you can at home, there would be little profit, but they would have no need to use chemical preservatives.

So much for commercial bakers. Let's turn our attention to the keeping of your bread.

KEEPING BREAD

The best way, bar none, to keep bread is in the freezer.

Bread is among the easiest and safest of foods to freeze, even for extended periods of time—up to a year, according to the United States Department of Agriculture.

There is virtually no loss of taste, texture, or wholesomeness in the frozen loaf, and, if you put it in the oven to reheat, it will come out tasting like the next best thing to fresh-baked.

To prepare bread for freezing, let it cool to room temperature. By doing this, we let dissipate whatever water vapor is being evaporated from the hot loaf before we wrap it, and minimize the water touching the crust.

I recommend wrapping the loaf tightly in aluminum foil for freezing. Then, on the happy day when you reheat, just put the loaf, foil and all, into the oven, and bake at high for about 10 minutes. It's amazing how good a loaf can be, even after it's been in your freezer for months.

You can use freezer paper, if you prefer, or even a tightly closed plastic bag. But then you must remove the loaf and put it on something to heat: you save a wash-up by using aluminum foil.

One thing about frozen bread: once thawed, it tends to go stale faster than fresh bread.

A bread gets *stale* (hard) as it loses its moisture. The moisture evaporates into the air while the other ingredients stay where they are, getting drier and drier, and harder and harder. A bread gets *moldy* because the microorganisms of this world find moist places (like bread) a good home to live in. These two problems, staleness and mold, are the two big difficulties in keeping bread fresh out of the freezer.

Let's attack the problem of loss of moisture—staleness—first. Believe it or not, bread retains its moisture best if it's quite warm. Again according to the USDA, bread will keep soft "indefinitely" (whatever that means) at 140° F. Now, that is warm. Just how would you do it? And if you could do it, how would you keep the mold away? Because mold absolutely loves temperatures like that.

The USDA also says that bread will keep soft for 100 hours (for those of you without adding machines, about four days) at 110° F. Also a nice breeding temperature for mold.

At 70° F., 40 hours (less than two days!).

How about putting bread into the refrigerator? We all know that's the reason we have refrigerators—to inhibit the growth of microorganisms. At 32° F., you can expect your bread to stay soft (fresh) for all of 10 hours.

That last figure came as a shock to me. I had been taught at my mother's knee (my mother had notoriously misinformed knees) to put unused bread in the fridge to keep it fresh. And now, the federal government was telling me that if I put my bread in the refrigerator I was just hurrying it to staleness.

So, any bread that isn't being frozen is best kept in a bread box. This will keep your breads at room temperature or slightly higher, and free from dust (though it does little for the problem of mold).

Breads vary greatly in keeping power. Those made with water get stale quickest. Honey will help a water bread keep its moisture (honey absorbs moisture from the air—your jar of honey will absorb moisture and thin out if you don't keep it tightly closed), and if you use enough honey you can keep a bread for weeks.

Shortening of any kind will help a bread stay moist (you know the way a drop of oil just won't dry out). The more shortening in a bread, the longer it will stay moist.

Of our breads, Brioches are the richest in oil: so oily that I can keep my treasure trove of Brioches in a plastic bag in the fridge for as long as 2 or 3 weeks without their going dry. At any weak moment I just pop one or two into my ancient top-of-the-stove potato baker, and, *voilà*, almost like fresh-baked.

But with any bread that uses shortening you run into another problem—rancidity.

Never eat anything rancid—if only the slightest bit. Rancid oils will destroy vitamins—they can also make you damn sick. So, if something sniffs *off*, throw it out. The money loss is not to be compared to the health loss.

Breads that are high in oil can be kept longer in the fridge without going hard. But I still recommend the freezer.

As for plastic bags, if still-warm breads are put in them their crusts are softened by their own moisture release. We like our crusts crusty, so if warm bread is to be kept overnight, or to be given to friends, we put it into a brown paper bag, folding the top several times to make it creature-proof, and let it get one day "stale" to protect the crust. Brown paper lets all the moisture *out*, keeping the bread clean and dust-free.

When does the process of "stale" begin? In one sense, as soon as you put a bread in the oven. The very process of baking involves moisture loss. (If you want proof, weigh your pan before and after baking. The weight loss is water.) Your nose also confirms this. When breads get done, their odor becomes very strong. Well, that odor is the result of evaporation—you smell the bread because of moisture particles.

Reviving stale bread involves trying to retrieve some of the lost moisture. Sprinkle a little water over the stale bread and then place it in the oven or toaster, just until the moisture reaches its original level. Alternatively, place the dry bread in a wet paper bag in the oven.

STORING DOUGH

Unbaked dough is more perishable than bread, but it keeps better in the fridge. Its life in the freezer and its life in the fridge are about the same—2 to 3 weeks. I have kept dough in the refrigerator for over a month, then baked it into rolls, to find myself with a good texture but a very "winey" flavor. I wouldn't recommend it.

Much as I recommend freezing bread, I can't see any point to freezing dough. In the refrigerator, the yeast is still working, though slowly, and you can get an extra rise or so from the dough, which only improves the texture of the bread you bake from it. In fact, many bakers prefer to work with refrigerated dough, finding it easier to handle.

To keep dough in the refrigerator, just cover the bowl of dough with clear plastic. If the dough rises out of the bowl, punch it down and push it back.

If you want to freeze shaped unrisen loaves or rolls, just wrap them in greased plastic film and put them in the freezer. Many doughs with things in them, such as seeds, actually improve in flavor during the freezing.

On baking day, the full-sized loaf will take 5 to 6 hours to thaw and rise, so you can save time by moving it from the freezer to the refrigerator the night before

Rolls will only take 2 hours to thaw.

Unshaped dough can be frozen, too, but you'll have to thaw it before you can shape it.

BROWN-AND-SERVE ROLLS

These are very popular as convenience rolls, and you can make your own, very simply and inexpensively (not to mention healthily). Bake any recipe at low temperatures (250°–275°) for half an hour, just long enough to make sure all the yeast is killed and the shape is set. They will still be pale in color. These can be stored 2 weeks in the fridge and indefinitely in the freezer. When you want to have them, simply bake in a high (400°) oven until brown. (An egg glaze just before the second baking will give you beautiful results—but don't put that egg glaze on before you stick the rolls in the fridge. Raw egg is very perishable.)

Appendix B
Federal Standards
for Commercial
Bread

The following is excerpted from BAKERY PRODUCTS, DEFINITIONS AND STANDARDS under the FEDERAL FOOD, DRUG, AND COSMETIC ACT. A full copy can be obtained free from the Department of Health, Education, and Welfare local office in your area. It states what may go into commercially prepared bread and in what amounts. To my eye it's a real horror story.

This is not an unbiased view. I have cut out the figures describing amounts, and condensed and left out the less harmful and commonplace ingredients—though what may go into bread as "milk" and "eggs" is also surprising and frightening.

You'll see the word "harmless" occasionally used. I don't think it's out of place for me to remind you that cyclamates were considered "harmless" until subsequent investigation proved otherwise.

Even if the individual chemical names don't mean much to you, read on, remembering that *none of the ingredients shown in the following excerpts has to be listed on the label of the bread* (except for those ingredients in paragraphs 13 and 14).

PART 17—BAKERY PRODUCTS

Sec. 17.2 Enriched bread and enriched rolls . . .

(a) Each of the foods enriched bread, enriched rolls . . . conforms to the definition and standard of identity . . . prescribed by . . . 17.1 (a) and (c) [see below] except that: . . . [standards of enrichment follow]

(3) . . . may also contain as an optional ingredient added harmless calcium salts . . . [amounts]

(6) . . . As used in this section, the term "flour," unqualified, includes bromated flour and phosphated flour; the term "enriched flour" includes enriched bromated flour . . .

Sec. 17.1

(a) . . . the potassium bromate in any bromated flour used and the monocalcium phosphate in any phosphated flour used shall be deemed to be optional ingredients . . .

(1) (ii) Mono- and diglycerides of fat-forming fatty acids, propylene glycol mono- and diesters of fat-forming fatty acids . . . [amount]

(5) . . . glucose sirup, dried corn sirup, dried glucose sirup, nondiastatic dried malt sirup . . .

(6) (ii) Harmless preparations of enzymes obtained from Aspergillus oryzae or bromelain preparations . . . in a suitable harmless carrier but the quantity of any such carrier shall be no greater than reasonably necessary to effect a uniform mixture of the enzymes with the flour used.

(iii) Harmless preparations of α-amylases, obtained from Bacillus subtilis . . . quantity . . . reasonably necessary . . .

(11) Calcium sulfate, calcium lactate, calcium carbonate, dicalcium phosphate, ammonium phosphate, ammonium sulfate, ammonium chloride, or any combination of two or more . . . [amounts]

(12) (i) Potassium bromate, calcium bromate, potassium iodate, calcium iodate, calcium peroxide, or any combination of two or more . . . [amounts]

(ii) Azodicarbonamide . . . in a carrier consisting of starch . . . tricalcium phosphate may be added as an anticaking agent . . . [amount]

(13) (i) Monocalcium phosphate . . . [amount]

(ii) A vinegar . . . [amount]

(iii) Calcium propionate, sodium propionate, or any mixture of these . . . [amount]

(iv) Sodium diacetate . . . [amount]

(v) Lactic acid, in such quantity that the pH of the finished bread is not less than 4.5.

(14) Spice, with which may be included spice oil and spice extract.

(15) Polysorbate 60, calcium stearoyl-2-lactylate, lactylic stearate, sodium stearyl fumarate, succinylated monoglycerides, ethoxylated mono- and diglycerides, alone or in combination . . . [amounts]

(16) L-Cysteine (which may be added in the form of the hydrochloride salt, including hydrates thereof) . . . [amount]

If you are eating commercially baked bread, you are eating any or many of these ingredients.

☞ Index ☜

Note: *Recipe pages are indicated by italics.*

About the Authors

FLOSS DWORKIN has taught hundreds of women, men, and children—from cooking teachers to absolute beginners—to bake bread, as well as having taught crafts, knitting, dance, and even psychology.

STAN DWORKIN, a short-story writer and a creative health-food cook himself, learned to bake bread during the preparation of *Bake Your Own Bread*, testing out the recipes invented by Floss.

Both the Dworkins are enthusiastic horticulturalists, folk dancers, bicyclists, and campers.

SIGNET Books of Special Interest

SIGNET Books You Will Enjoy

☐ **THE I NEVER COOKED BEFORE COOKBOOK by Jo Coudert.** A basic guide in plain English on how to prepare simple, delicious foods with ease . . . and the certainty of success. No experience necessary.
(#Y5768—$1.25)

☐ **LET'S COOK IT RIGHT by Adelle Davis.** Competely revised and updated, this is the celebrated cookbook dedicated to good health, good sense and good eating. Contains 400 easy-to-follow, basic recipes, a table of equivalents and an index. (#E5378—$1.75)

☐ **THE EASY WAY TO CHINESE COOKING by Beverly Lee.** In this practical, easy-to-follow guide to authentic Chinese cooking, Beverly Lee shows how to make delicious Chinese dishes—from the simplest to the most festive and elaborate. Included is a list of Chinese stores throughout the U.S. which carry the items listed in the book. (#Q4813—95¢)

☐ **THE GOURMET'S GUIDE TO MEAT AND POULTRY by William and Chesbrough Rayner.** In a world where meat prices keep getting higher and quality is constantly being questioned, only the person who can judge cuts of meat can afford to buy meat. This book will show you how you can stretch your budget and turn inexpensive cuts of meat into delicious, nutritious meals.
(#Q4783—95¢)

☐ **EVERYDAY FRENCH COOKING by Henri-Paul Pellaprat.** A former Cordon Bleau professor has written an easy-to-use, complete French cookbook. (#E6016—$1.75)

THE NEW AMERICAN LIBRARY, INC.,
P.O. Box 999, Bergenfield, New Jersey 07621

Please send me the SIGNET BOOKS I have checked above. I am enclosing $_____(check or money order—no currency or C.O.D.'s). Please include the list price plus 25¢ a copy to cover handling and mailing costs. (Prices and numbers are subject to change without notice.)

Name_____

Address_____

City_____State_____Zip Code_____
Allow at least 3 weeks for delivery